Using the Law Library

*Your Guide to Legal Resources
In (and Outside) the Law Library*

© 2004

Also by HALT:

Using a Lawyer

Do-it-Yourself Law

The Legal Resource Directory

If You Want to Sue a Lawyer

The Easy Way to Probate

Your Guide to Living Trusts & Other Trusts

Wills

Small Claims Court

Legal Rights for Seniors

The Smart Consumer

Everyday Contracts

A CITIZENS LEGAL MANUAL

Using the Law Library

*Your Guide to Legal Resources
In (and Outside) the Law Library*

**Updated by HALT and Jennifer Sekula
of the Marshall-Wythe Law Library,
College of William & Mary School of Law**

AN ORGANIZATION OF
AMERICANS FOR LEGAL REFORM

Author (Third Edition): HALT and Jennifer Sekula
Design & Production: Barking Dog Design/Chris McGee
Substantial Assistance Provided By: Chris Byrne, Amy Dieterich,
Jeff Goodnow, Thomas Gordon, Jim Heller, Victoria Oliver, Kyle Rice,
Theresa Meehan Rudy and Kristin Weber.

The original draft of this book was authored by Paul Hasse and
Adrian Helm. Substantial assistance with the 1988 edition was provided by
George Milko, Michael Kress, Richard Hebert, Kay Ostberg, David Bell,
Lisa Jacobsen, Aleas N. Jones, Claudette Straughter and Liberty Swift.

Print History:

First Edition
1st printing—1982
2nd printing—1983

Second Edition
1st printing—1988
2nd printing—1999

Third Edition
1st printing—2004

ISBN 0-910073-27-9

Contents

ACKNOWLEDGMENTS

We would like to gratefully express our appreciation to the following individuals and organizations for their support in making this book possible:

Danielle Brian, Katherine S. Broderick, Robert & Amy Charles Family Foundation, Louis A. Clark, Edward Dempsey, Dreammaker Foundation, Catherine Elias-Jermany, Ethan Grossman Family Charitable Gift Fund, Ferro 1986 Revocable Trust, The Fund for Constitutional Government, The Wallace Alexander Gerbode Foundation, The Government Accountability Project, Paul and Victoria Hasse, Hendricks Foundation, Jon Legallet, Kimmel Family Foundation, Conrad Martin, McMillion Foundation, George A. Miller, the Modzelewski Charitable Trust, Stewart R. Mott Charitable Trust, Beatrice Moulton, William C. & Gloria A. Newton, Onodera Family Trust, Project on Government Oversight, David & Marian Rocker, San Francisco Foundation, Suzanne Sloat & Ray Okonski Foundation, Jack Taylor Family Foundation, Inc., S.J. Ungar & J. Shapiro Family Foundation, Inc.

HALT, Inc.
January 2004

Foreword

When HALT began, one of its first educational efforts was a plain-language guide called **Using the Law Library**. Compiled by HALT founder Paul Hasse, this guide demystified the process of legal research and provided step-by-step instructions on how to find and use legal precedent.

Over the years, **Using the Law Library** has been one of HALT's most popular publications, with bulk orders even coming from law schools that use it as a textbook in their first year legal research and writing courses.

With the advent of the Internet and online research tools, there are now new resources for those looking for help with their legal questions. But to be fully empowered, consumers should also be able to use the resources that are readily available in law libraries across the country. Whether located in a court, at a college or in a law school, these libraries can provide the detailed information about statutes, rules, regulations and court decisions that together make up our system of laws.

This expanded Third Edition of **Using the Law Library: Your Guide to Legal Resources In (and Outside) the Law Library** has been updated by HALT and Jennifer Sekula of the Marshall-Wythe Law Library, College of William & Mary School of Law. This new edition not only provides the basic nuts and bolts of library-based research, it also guides consumers to other resources that can help them make more effective use of the law library.

For a quarter century, HALT has worked to help ordinary Americans take charge of their own legal affairs, and the book you hold in your hands is an integral part of this education and reform effort. Together with two other HALT *Citizens Legal Manuals*, **Courts & Judges** and **The Legal Resource Directory: Your Guide to Help, Hotlines & Hot Websites,** this book can help you understand how our court system works and how to find the answers to your legal questions.

These *Citizens Legal Manuals* are also designed to be used in concert with the regularly updated Legal Information Clearinghouse pages of HALT's Internet site, *www.halt.org*. There, visitors can find HALT's *Everyday Law Series* and other self-help materials, up-to-date links to legal resources on the Internet and a wealth of other consumer information.

Whether you use this book to help you conduct research on a specific legal issue or consult it to learn more about the resources available to help you deal with legal decisions, remember the most important job is still up to you—you are the one person who can take charge of your own legal affairs. We hope that the information in this book and our efforts at HALT will help you do so.

James C. Turner

Executive Director
HALT—*An Organization of Americans for Legal Reform*
Washington, DC

January 2004

Introduction

Using the Law Library is a guide to help you use the resources in (and outside) a law library to answer legal questions. It is written for non-lawyers who want to answer specific questions or research an area of the law. The process developed for this manual is designed to help nonlawyers answer basic legal questions.

There is no reason to feel as though a nonlawyer can't do legal research. Although much of the material that you will use is not written in plain English, a good legal dictionary and some patience and determination are all you need to get answers to most legal questions.

This manual allows you to investigate each of the many sources that may contain the answers you seek. Some of those resources may even be located outside the law library; for example, online or through a self-help legal publication. But before you start looking for answers to your legal questions, this book will first teach you about the different types of of law, how they are created and how they interact. In fact, some chapters are devoted entirely to describing how our legal system works. This is because if you don't know how the system works, you cannot know where to begin or end your research or know what kind of law covers your particular legal question. For a more detailed discussion of our court system, refer to HALT's *Citizens Legal Manual*, **Courts & Judges.**

Other chapters in this manual explain how to use standard legal reference materials. This often requires detailed, step-by-step explanations of how to use the index of one set of volumes or the update services of another. Many of these explanations will be easier to understand when you are actually using the books in a library. As with dancing or bicycling, reading about legal research is not the same as trying to do it. There is no substitute for experience. This manual can be used most effectively as you actually work with the reference materials it describes.

HOW TO USE THIS BOOK

Read the first five chapters before you go to a law library. You will save time if you also read the remaining chapters for an overview of the research process. Do not, however, spend much time trying to follow the step-by-step instructions in each chapter without a copy of the appropriate reference book before you.

A complete reading of this manual will demonstrate that legal research has many possible starting points and many potential dead ends. The process we suggest starts at the most general level and proceeds down different paths to specific types of information. It may be that you can answer your questions with the most basic reference material, such as a legal encyclopedia. On the other hand, your question may be so unusual or specific that you will have to exhaust every possible reference source by digging through cases and statutes.

The rules for using the manual are simple: follow the research path described and stop when you are satisfied you have all the information you need. After you've learned how to use the basic resources in a law library, the most difficult task will be knowing when to stop. Figuring out when you have located the most recent, relevant and authoritative information is largely a product of experience. It's the experience that comes from following many leads in many resource materials.

You will eventually learn to recognize false leads but, in the meantime, don't take chances by looking for shortcuts. You may reach Chapter 9 and discover that you have had the correct answer since Chapter 6, but the additional time spent in research is an investment in certainty. In legal research, an incomplete answer is the wrong answer.

THE LIMITS OF LEGAL RESEARCH

This manual is only a tool, and all tools are limited in their uses. The limits of this manual are obvious: it tells you everything most nonlawyers need to know in order to answer common legal questions, but it does not tell you everything there is to know about legal research. That would take hundreds of pages to explain. Some of the best books on the subject are included in Appendix I.

This manual can be misused only if you expect too much of it or of legal research in general. It is not a litigation manual. It will not tell you how to take a case to court. Legal research can give you answers to basic questions, such as: "What are the grounds for suing a business for breaking a contract in New Jersey?" What it can't answer conclusively, however, is a question like: "Will I win if I sue a New Jersey shipper for failing to deliver perishable goods to me by the promised date?"

Legal research can tell you if people in similar situations have won their suits against shippers in New Jersey, and it may tell you why they won or lost. If people have won similar suits in the past, then there may be established reasons (or precedent) why you should win. But taking legal action is always a percentage game. The statute may read in your favor, but years of case decisions may have created exceptions that apply in cases like yours.

Legal research tells you what the law says and how it has been interpreted by the courts. It can give you the information you need to decide whether to go to court and to understand what might happen to you there. It can answer many questions about uncontested matters, and it can even indicate the odds of your winning in court—if nothing goes wrong. With this manual and the realization that the decisions are ultimately yours to make, you may even find legal research to be a rewarding experience!

Using the Law Library

Your Guide to Legal Resources
In (and Outside) the Law Library

CHAPTER 1

Some Basics

Before beginning any kind of legal research, it is important to have a solid understanding of the entire process and to learn a few pointers acquired by others from years of research experience. This chapter provides that information.

LAW FOR THE NONLAWYER

Often you can benefit from others' research by looking for books, cassette tapes, CDs, or computer software produced on many legal subjects by an ever growing number of legal self-help publishers. See **Do-it-Yourself Law: HALT's Guide to Self-Help Books, Kits & Software,** which evaluates more than 50 do-it-yourself publications. These do-it-yourself materials are written for nonlawyers in plain language. If you find one on your subject, you may discover all your work has been done for you. Many of these materials are also state-specific. For instance, Nolo in Berkeley, California, publishes *Your Rights in the Workplace,* a book that answers questions about employment law and gives state-by-state breakdowns of specific laws, such as whistleblower protections.

Try to answer your questions using these materials first. Some law libraries have a section called "Law for the Layperson" or "Self-Help." Many public libraries and bookstores have even wider selections.

LAWYER HANDBOOKS

A second shortcut is to do what lawyers do—look for a handbook or manual on your subject. It may substantially reduce your research by answering the most frequently-asked questions. For instance, a local bar association that has an immigration section may have published a manual on how to apply for permanent-resident status, which may tell you all you need to know.

The problem is that these handbooks are hard to find and are not generally available to nonlawyers. Most are published by sections of state and local bar associations, by national bar associations whose members have a common interest in one area of law or by legal services or legal aid organizations that publish them to help their own lawyers.

Try looking for these in a library or ask a lawyer friend if you can borrow any such materials that cover your subject. Because they are written for practicing attorneys, though, they may be less likely to be part of a research library's collection. *(The various types of law libraries are discussed in Chapter 2.)*

Continuing Legal Education materials are a related type of manual that may be easier to find in some libraries. These are also produced for lawyers, but they are intended to explain specific areas of the law to attorneys who may not be current on the subject. Therefore, while often narrow in scope, Continuing Legal Education materials (usually in a binder or book format) lay out the current state of the law on that topic, present step-by-step instructions and sometimes include forms as well.

PRIMARY AND SECONDARY SOURCES

Throughout this book, you will see the terms *primary* and *secondary* sources. Primary sources are the elements that make up our law: case opinions, statutes, constitutions, executive orders and administrative rules and regulations. In other words, they are the law.

Secondary sources are descriptions or interpretations of those primary materials. They can be annotated versions of statutes that explain their meanings and histories, a legal encyclopedia divided by area of law, a journal article or a practice and procedure book. While not the law itself, these sources explain what the law is and how it has been applied.

We suggest that you start with secondary sources and use the references you find in them to get to the primary sources. It is always important (and sometimes required) to cite primary sources when you are referring to the law in court or in a legal document.

The beauty of using secondary sources first is that their discussions are organized to get you to the point faster than primary sources like cases and statutes. Judicial opinions and statutes, by contrast, often require you to wade through a lot of irrelevant material before you find the information you're looking for. Secondary sources will provide the answer to the vast majority of legal questions and do so faster.

THE U.S. SYSTEM

Any research effort *must* begin with an understanding of the structure of the U.S. legal system. Otherwise, you may find yourself quoting law that has been overruled by a higher authority. Think of the law as deriving from three sources—courts, legislatures and the executive branch of government. These three branches and their relationships are discussed in the next chapter. For now, you need remember only that courts interpret statutes passed by the legislature and rules or regulations issued by the executive branch of government.

HOW COURTS OPERATE

The U.S. has two basic court systems: the federal courts and 50 state court systems. They are separate, and whether your case is heard in one or the other is a complex matter discussed throughout this manual, especially in Chapters 4 and 9 through 14.

Courts operate by issuing opinions. Each opinion has a holding on the issue the court considered. Together, these holdings make up what is called precedent. Precedent governs and guides other courts when they are faced with deciding a case with similar facts. The holdings of a court govern until a higher court overrules them.

Consider this example: a state enacts a law making it illegal for "publicly-financed" hospitals to deny medical treatment to people who have no health insurance. Someone who has no insurance is denied treatment and sues a hospital that gets half its funds from the state. The question is whether this hospital is considered publicly-financed and covered by the law. The court rules that it is not covered, reasoning that only hospitals that receive *more than* half of their funding from the state are considered "publicly-financed" within the meaning of the statute. Therefore no violation of the statute occurred in this case. This ruling becomes precedent for all other cases with similar facts.

If, however, the person appealed and a higher court determined that a hospital that receives *exactly* half its money from the state is, in fact, a "publicly-financed" hospital, then the lower court is overruled and all cases in the future will be guided by this new precedent. In doing your research, therefore, it is always important to look to the most recent precedent from higher courts.

CHAPTER 2

Finding a Library

To begin your legal research, you must have access to a law library. Your local public library, unless it is in a major metropolitan area, probably does not have the large number of legal materials you'll need to make your research thorough. Some Web sites, such as *www.findlaw.com*, contain thousands of legal sites, cases, codes, forms and other information that may help you get started. For in-depth legal research, however, you need a law library.

TYPES OF LAW LIBRARIES

Law libraries come in two types—research law libraries and working law libraries.

Research law libraries usually contain more books than working law libraries. Law schools have research libraries. A typical library of this type has a collection that includes legal journals and law reviews, case reporters, state and federal statutes and scholarly works. Research law libraries may also have significant international law collections with books and journals offering in-depth examinations of the legal systems of other nations. They also feature numerous online databases that contain up-to-date indexes and possibly full-text documents.

A working law library usually has fewer volumes. A typical one may have case-law reports from some jurisdictions, some state and federal statutes and administrative regulations. Working law libraries also usually have some basic secondary sources (encyclopedias, digests, journals, form books and treatises designed for the use of lawyers). In a working law library, expect to find substantially fewer journals, treatises and loose-leaf services than in a research library. Also, the number of freely available online resources may be quite limited.

Research law libraries are intended for legal scholars and law students, while working law libraries contain only those materials attorneys and judges need for practicing law. Both types of libraries contain the sources you'll need, but working law libraries contain fewer support materials to help you. They also have fewer of the easier-to-use secondary sources. On the other hand, research libraries may lack some of the products designed only for practitioners, though this is generally not much of a handicap.

Working law libraries are designed for those who are already familiar with the basics of law. Research law libraries, because they contain everything from the most basic to the most sophisticated materials, offer a more hospitable environment for the novice legal researcher.

LOCATING A LAW LIBRARY

Depending where you live, you may have a choice between a research law library and a working law library. On the other hand, you may have difficulty locating any law library near you. Research law libraries are typically found only in law schools, a few major metropolitan public libraries and the Library of Congress in Washington, D.C. State law libraries can house major collections, though state and federal courthouse libraries are not usually as large as research law libraries. These types of libraries are usually complete, lacking only the most basic introductory materials and the more subject-specific academic studies. In some states, such as Virginia and Louisiana, a court library serves as the state law library.

City and county courthouses usually have standard working law libraries. County law libraries tend to be more complete and are much more common than city libraries, but libraries in large cities are usually larger than those of the counties in which they are located. Both city and county law libraries usually contain only those materials relevant to their state, plus a limited collection of federal statutes and case-law materials.

Law offices often have private law libraries that, in the largest firms, may feature an impressive collection. In many locations, small practitioners pool their resources and establish a law library for all the residents of a particular office building or for members of a private bar association. Large corporations with full-time legal staffs may also have in-house law libraries, but these are often highly specialized. In general, though, law firm libraries are shrinking as lawyers elect to use electronic versions of traditionally printed material.

As a last resort, non-law libraries such as public and university libraries usually have some basic materials about the law. Both contain general introductory works and a few primary and secondary legal resources, including the state's statutory code. The public library can be particularly helpful in researching your city's charter, code or municipal ordinances. However, public libraries sometimes do not update their legal reference sources, so be particularly careful to check that you are using the most recent resource material available.

Finding a law library near you is actually fairly simple. Public, university, law school and courthouse libraries can be found in the telephone book. Law libraries that you may not know about may also be located in the next county or within a government office in your city. To make sure you have a complete list of law libraries in your area, visit a large public library and look through the *Law and Legal Information Directory*, the *AALL Directory and Handbook* or the *Subject Directory of Special Libraries and Information Centers*. To get you started, this manual includes a partial list of law libraries in Appendix IV. Additional libraries can be found online by searching *"law libraries and directory"* using a general search engine such as Google or Yahoo.

RULES FOR PUBLIC USE

Some law school libraries are open to the public. Because these are research law libraries, they should be your first choice. A large number of law school libraries must open at least part of their collection to the public because they have been designated as *Federal Depository Libraries.*

Because these libraries have been granted the privilege of receiving a free copy of U.S. Government publications, they must make these publications available for the free use of the general public. Because of the difficulty involved in segregating these materials from the remainder of the library's collection and the organizational inconsistencies it would create, some of these libraries make their other reference materials available for public use as well. A library may, however, have the federal materials pulled from the shelves and brought to a non-student enclosed area.

Those law libraries currently designated as government depository libraries are noted with asterisks (*) in Appendix IV. If you are refused access to any of the government publications in these libraries, contact the Joint Committee on Printing in the U.S. Congress at (202) 225-8281. Most law school libraries have the additional advantage of being open at night and on weekends. Be cautioned, however, that many law schools permit only their faculty and students to use the library during exam time (in December and April/May), but even then you may be able to get in if you make a special request to the librarian.

If you can't find a law school library you can use, you might try the statehouse or a federal or state courthouse. Whether they are open to the public depends on both the rules set by the courthouse administrator and the consent of the librarian on duty.

Informal admissions policies are even more common in county and city courthouse libraries. Some states (such as California and Connecticut) require that county courthouse libraries be open to the public, but most states' laws are either vague or ignore the issue. In some county courthouses, the county provides a room for the law library, but the county bar association buys the books and operates the library.

Access to a county or city courthouse law library is often subject to "special permission." The only way to find out if you can use such a courthouse library is to speak with a librarian. Explain that you have a particular question of law that you want to research, that you are familiar with the basic resource materials and that you will observe all the rules of conduct for users of the library. If a letter from an attorney is also required, visit the prosecutor's or public defender's office in the court house, explain what you want to research in the library and politely request a letter or note on your behalf.

With the exception of law school and some state law libraries, most law libraries are open only 9 a.m. to 5 p.m., Monday through Friday. A few courthouse libraries are open on Saturdays, but they are the exception. Always call a law library or check its Web site to confirm its hours and rules for access before you make the trip.

The law libraries of law firms, attorneys' office buildings and bar associations are privately-owned and are not open to the general public. However, a letter from a local attorney may get you into a bar association's library.

In sum, whether the library admits the public is not always predictable. Despite the generalities presented here, admissions policies will vary from library to library. Once you have located one near you, the best thing to do is simply check the library's Web site or call and ask about its policies.

LIBRARY STAFF

In order to use a library most efficiently, you should figure out who among the staff, if anyone, can help you. Whether you need directions to the copier or you can't find a book on your topic, it is helpful to understand how a library is staffed. Smaller libraries may employ only one or two people, while in larger ones, you may find dozens of staff members.

Not everyone who works in a library is a librarian. Law libraries are often comprised of several levels of staff, from part-time pages and clerks to the director of the library. Librarians have special skills (and usually a degree as well) in information science. Reference librarians are trained to assist library users in finding what they're looking for, and will be able to help you the most throughout your research. If the library is large enough to have them (and most research libraries are), be sure to ask for a reference librarian when you get to the library or when you are stuck in your research. A non-reference librarian can assist you as well, as can the general staff, but a reference librarian who deals with the collection and patrons every day is your best bet for good research advice.

Some law schools offer clinics that offer legal assistance to certain types of people in certain types of situations. Be careful, though, about consulting non-library staff for help. Students or other researchers that you run across in the library cannot help you with your research, nor should you ask them to. Not only are they unfamiliar with the nuances of the law pertaining to your situation, but Unauthorized Practice of Law statutes prevent them from giving more than the most general research advice.

CHAPTER 3

Library Rules

Now that you know something about the types of law libraries, here are a few simple tips to keep in mind when using one. Some are purely practical—things that will prevent you from being unprepared (or unwelcome) once you are in the library. Others are tactical—tips that will make the research process easier and will help you avoid making mistakes or wasting time.

1. Call the library to verify its hours. Don't try to begin your legal research an hour (or even two hours) before closing. Ask about photocopying and whether a change machine is available. Also ask whether the library's machines take change or whether you have to purchase a special card from which the price of each copy is deducted automatically. Find out what the policy is regarding computer use and the Internet and whether public printing is available.

2. Take along plenty of paper or index cards, pens or pencils, change for the copying machine (if needed), a floppy disk (if downloading from computer is available) and—of course—this manual. Printing from computers may be limited, though you can sometimes E-mail your search results to yourself.

3. If you need the librarian's consent to use the library, begin by introducing yourself to the librarian. Explain what you want to do and ask if it matters where you sit.

4. Ask for a map of the library. If none is available, a librarian or other staff member may offer a brief tour or explanation.

5. Ask for the reference librarian on duty, if there is one, or for any available librarian if the library you're using doesn't have specialists. A brief con-

versation at the beginning of your research may save you hours of fruitless digging. Librarians are usually quite willing to help nonlawyers, but some do not deal with the public on a regular basis. They will help you locate the resources you need, but cannot do your research for you or interpret what you find—Unauthorized Practice of Law statutes forbid them from doing so. Also, ask a librarian for help as soon as you discover that you need it.

6. If possible, find a work space near a law dictionary so you can easily look up Latin words and other phrases you come across. You may want to bring a law dictionary written for nonlawyers with you. We recommend *The Dictionary of Legal Terms*, available from HALT. Other useful dictionaries include *Real Life Dictionary of the Law*, *Law Dictionary for Nonlawyers* or *Random House Webster's Dictionary of the Law*.

7. Be methodical and use common sense. As you read through this manual, make an outline or list of the sources you want to consult. You may find it's a useful summary of steps to follow in your research.

8. Write down complete information about each source before you begin to take notes from it. Include the date of publication, along with the volume, section and page numbers. If using an online source, note its name, how you got to it, and which parts of it you used. It is extremely important that your notes contain specific references to the materials you use. This will save you hours if you have to return to the source at a later date. It will also allow you to remember what you have already consulted in case you cannot complete your research in a single sitting.

9. Always read the prefaces, content descriptions and instructions of the resource materials that you use. This takes a few minutes, but it can save you hours of fruitless research through a source that is of no value to you.

10. Locate and put a bookmark in the abbreviations tables found in the front of many secondary sources. Deciphering abbreviations is time-consuming enough without also having to hunt for this table each time.

11. When you see a reference to another source that might be helpful, write down all of the citation information—all of the abbreviations, the numbers and the publication date. Also, make a note of why you were referred to that source. Even if you are not sure that you will need the information, you can't afford to lose valuable clues in the early stages of research.

12. Don't let it overwhelm you. When you are tired, give yourself a break. Legal research can be exhausting, and it requires complete concentration and attention to detail if you are to be successful. Take one step at a time, do not take risky shortcuts and don't rush.

13. Take only the books you need from the shelves, and take them only as you need them. A sure sign of the novice researcher is dozens of books stacked on the table. Other people will be using the library, and it is a great nuisance to them when important reference books are missing from the shelves for long periods of time.

14. When you are finished with a book, put it back where it belongs. Some libraries want you to return the books to the shelves. Others have a special cart or table for books that are to be reshelved. If it isn't obvious, be sure to ask the librarian where you should leave books when you're finished.

15. Thank the librarian or other staff members as you leave. Making a good impression will make it easier for you and other nonlawyers to use the library next time.

CHAPTER 4

The U.S. System

This chapter is more than a civics course: it contains specific information you must know to find the law you're looking for. Where you find the law will depend entirely on both the type of law and its source.

There are five types of law: *constitutional, legislative* or *statutory, executive, administrative* and *judicial* or *case* law. These may all be made at the local, state or federal levels. Most primary legal resources contain only one type of law from one particular level of government. For instance, one set of volumes may report only federal court cases. Another may just report state administrative law. To find the law you want, it is essential that you know from which branch of government it was issued. To know that, you need to understand the basic make-up of the executive, legislative and judicial branches of government at the federal, state and local levels.

Your legal questions may concern state statutes and interpretative state court decisions. Legal issues such as divorce and domestic problems, wills and probate and landlord-tenant law are all traditionally handled at the state level. On the other hand, some issues like labor and employment disputes are governed by both federal and state law. Some legal questions, such as antitrust issues and communications law, are handled only at the federal level.

THREE BRANCHES AT THREE LEVELS

Think of the government as a tree with three tiers of branches (federal, state and local), all of which have some authority to make laws. At each tier, there are three branches: the executive, the legislative and the judicial.

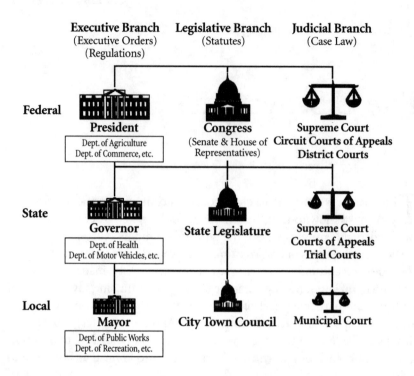

Federal Government. Based in Washington, D.C., the federal executive branch consists of the president and the many administrative departments and agencies, such as the Department of Commerce, the Environmental Protection Agency and the Social Security Administration. The legislative branch of the federal government is the Congress, which writes statutes for the country. Finally, a federal judicial branch consists of a Supreme Court, 13 Circuit Courts of Appeals, 94 District Courts and some special-purpose courts.

State Government. State governments operate similarly, with an executive branch headed by a governor and consisting of many departments, such as the departments of Health or Motor Vehicles; a state legislature, called the Assembly or something similar, which writes state laws; and a state judicial branch, consisting of a high court and a number of inferior courts.

Local Government. Local governments have counterparts to all of the above. A local executive branch may be headed by a mayor, city manager or county executive and include such departments as Recreation and Public Works. The local legislature will be called a city, county or town council, a board of supervisors or something similar. Cities sometimes have their own courts.

Together, all the levels and branches either directly write the laws or interpret them in a way that, in effect, makes law.

HOW THEY RELATE

Within one level of government, the executive and legislative branches are "co-equal." Each may create binding law on just about any issue that concerns its constituents, unless forbidden from doing so by a constitution or higher law.

Among the different *levels* of government, however, certain subject areas are reserved either by the constitution or by tradition to one level or the other. For instance, the U.S. Constitution requires that only the president, and not a governor, can negotiate treaties with other countries and that only the U.S. Bureau of Printing and Engraving, not a state agency, can coin money. Conversely, the states have traditionally retained authority to make laws about education.

In instances when both the state government and the federal government exercise authority over the same area, if there is a conflict, the federal government's laws usually prevail.

The relationship between the state and federal levels is not so clear-cut when it comes to courts. Why a case is in one or the other court's *jurisdiction* is discussed in great detail in Chapter 12. For now, it is enough to understand the structures involved.

A DUAL SYSTEM

Each state has its own system of courts, which operates alongside the federal court system.

The U.S. Constitution reflects the efforts of its framers to balance the competing interests of autonomy for individual states and a strong central government. Accordingly, the power of the federal courts, like federal legislative and executive authority, is limited to those powers listed in the Constitution or specified in legislation passed by Congress. Typical among cases that can be brought in federal court are lawsuits against the U.S. government and cases involving the application of federal law.

Other types of cases that can be brought at the federal level are those that involve diversity jurisdiction where the amount in dispute does not exceed $75,000 (as of August 2003). When a lawsuit involves two or more citizens of different states and involves state law, the federal courts can hear such a case.

For more information about diversity jurisdiction, see Chapter 12.

The powers of state governments extend to all matters that the U.S. Constitution does not reserve to the federal government. Typical state cases include accident claims, family disputes, traffic matters and non-federal crimes.

The following is a general outline of the *sources* of the law—how various laws came to be. Directions concerning how to research a particular type of law in a law library will be given in succeeding chapters.

CONSTITUTIONAL LAW

Constitutional law is found in the U.S. Constitution, the constitutions of the various states and municipal constitutions, often called charters.

The U.S. Constitution. The U.S. Constitution is the supreme law of the land. No law, treaty or administrative ruling is valid unless it is consistent with current legal interpretation of the Constitution. The Constitution can only be changed by an amendment that has been approved by three-fourths of the states' legislatures.

In a series of case rulings (principally a case called *Marbury v. Madison,* in 1803), the U.S. Supreme Court established itself as the final authority in deciding whether or not a particular law or action conforms with the Constitution. Both the Congress (the legislative branch) and the president (the executive branch) acquiesced in the court's claim, and, since then, the Supreme Court has defined the limits of governmental action according to the "mandate of the people" in the U.S. Constitution.

It is important to understand the full implication of the U.S. Constitution's role as "the supreme law of the land." No ordinary congressional statute or presidential act may override it. All state and municipal constitutions and statutes are inferior to it. The U.S. Constitution is the bedrock of American law, and the U.S. Supreme Court is the final arbiter of what that Constitution means.

The U.S. Constitution is always subject to reinterpretation by the Supreme Court and, to a lesser extent, lower courts. The words of the Constitution have been reinterpreted many times over the years. In doing your research, never rely on the mere words of any constitution or statute. It is the interpretation applied in court cases that matters.

State Constitutions. After the U.S. Constitution, a state's constitution is supreme *within that state's borders.* Its relation to state law is comparable to the U.S. Constitution's relation to federal law. As with the U.S. Constitution, a state constitution is a grant of limited power to the state by its citizens. But no valid provision of a state constitution may violate federal constitutional law. State constitutions are also usually inferior to all U.S. treaties and federal statutes.

Municipal Charters. A municipal charter is, in effect, the "constitution" for a city or town. It is superior to all ordinances enacted by the municipality, but inferior to all state and federal laws. Municipal charters are granted by a state legislative enactment or by a state constitution's "home rule" provision. In a municipal charter, the state transfers or "grants" certain governmental powers to a local entity, such as a city council. Like other constitutions, a municipal charter is a permission to rule under specific terms set by the state.

LEGISLATIVE OR STATUTORY LAW

The second kind of law is *legislative* or *statutory*. A statute is simply a formal enactment by a legislative body. U.S. statutes are enacted by the U.S. Congress and signed by the president; state statutes are adopted by the state legislatures and signed by the governor; and municipal ordinances are passed by the city council and signed by the mayor.

A constitution gives a government a specific structure, a specified amount of power and certain general goals. For example, the Preamble to the U.S. Constitution states that it is the duty of the federal government to "insure domestic tranquility, provide for the common defense, [and] promote the general welfare." Legislative bodies routinely face the dilemma of how to accomplish their goals within the limits of their constitutional authority. Their policy decisions with regard to rules for social behavior, governmental expenditures, enforcement of constitutional guarantees and so forth are published as statutes. When people speak of "the law" and mean a law passed by Congress or a state legislature, they are referring to a statute.

U.S. Statutes. U.S. statutes are the laws enacted by the U.S. Congress. They are inferior only to the U.S. Constitution and usually override all other law. They can be found in a number of places, as discussed in Chapter 10.

State Statutes. State statutes are enacted by state legislatures and are binding within a state's borders if they are not in conflict with existing federal law or the state's constitution.

Some states publish a complete edition of all statutes in force at the end of each legislative session. Other states publish at wider intervals and issue only year-end summaries (called "Session Laws" or "Acts of Assembly") for the intervening years. Some states do not publish their collected statutes at all, but designate a private publisher's version as "official."

Municipal Ordinances. Municipal ordinances are a city's statutes, enacted by its governing body. The method of enactment varies, depending on the city's charter. Municipal ordinances are inferior to all state and federal laws. They are printed by the local government that enacts them, but distribution (especially in smaller communities) may be limited.

EXECUTIVE MATERIALS AND ADMINISTRATIVE LAW

Administrative law includes the rules and decisions of government agencies as well as proclamations issued by the chief executive of the government (such as executive orders). However, for research purposes, it is often helpful to separate the two—primarily because of the ways in which they are published.

Both executive materials and administrative law issue from the executive branches of the federal, state and local governments. In this manual, executive materials will refer to executive orders and proclamations by the president, state governors and mayors which have the effect of law. Administrative law will be used to refer to agency or department regulations or decisions in disputes over those regulations, called rulings.

When state and federal agencies share responsibility for regulation (as in alcohol or firearm regulations), state executive and administrative laws that are involved are inferior to federal executive and administrative law. If municipal executive or administrative laws are involved, they are inferior to both state and federal laws of all kinds.

The importance of regulations cannot be over-emphasized. They govern both procedural and substantive questions. For example, federal Social Security regulations define the time during which a claimant can bring an appeal (a procedural issue) *and* the medical standards that she must meet to obtain disability benefits under the program (a substantive issue).

The *Federal Register* and state regulatory reporters publish administrative decisions. Also, some agencies publish plain-language descriptions of their regulations.

JUDICIAL OR CASE LAW

The United States system is based on *common law*. Because the enacted statutes do not cover every dispute that might arise, disputes that are not covered are governed by the common law—the vast collected history of cases decided by courts in the past. Statutory law is also usually general in its wording, and judges are frequently called upon to decide how this general law should be applied in specific cases. What results is common law, often a necessary supplement to the understanding of statutory law.

More often, this is called *case law*. Judges issue opinions on the cases they hear, and these become the law on that particular topic.

Common law is the product of a history of court decisions. That is, by consistently treating similar cases in a similar way, certain rules for judicial decision-making become "laws" in themselves. Again, the principles set out in earlier case decisions are called precedent.

Precedent. The courts use precedent to build stability and order into the judicial system by treating similar problems in a consistent manner. They follow a principle known as *stare decisis,* meaning "to stand by things decided." In effect, previous decisions make up the constraints and guidelines that a court will follow when deciding a new case. To find out what the law (the common law) is in a given area, it is necessary to read the opinions and reasoning of judges who have dealt with similar issues in the past. If the previous cases are truly similar in nature to yours, then the decisions of the previous judges should be used to guide (but not necessarily dictate) the decision of your judge. The process of finding analogous cases from the past and convincing a judge that this precedent should be followed is what legal research to prepare a case is all about. This is why lawyers cite previous cases in their briefs.

Jurisdiction. In general, state courts hear cases involving state law, and federal courts hear cases involving federal laws, treaties, the U.S. Constitution and disputes between citizens of different states. Because the decisions made by a state court apply only in its jurisdiction, each state has its own case law and common law history. The same is also true of the federal court system.

The *jurisdiction* of a court defines which cases it may and may not consider. This is decided in three ways: by geography, by type of case and by whether a court is the first to hear the case or receives it only on appeal.

First, each court has a geographical district. It may not consider cases involving disputes that occur outside the boundaries of that district. A county court hears cases that involve residents or incidents that occur within the county. The highest court in a state is limited by the boundaries of that state. The federal court system is itself divided into 94 districts and 13 circuits, each limited to cases within certain geographic boundaries. Furthermore, the court must have personal jurisdiction, meaning that the parties must have some connection with the district in order to fall under its court's jurisdiction. For example, if a person has conducted no activity within a given state and has no ties to it, that state will most likely be unable to require that person to appear in its courts as a defendant. If the case involves property that is located within the court's geographic area, the court exercises a special kind of personal jurisdiction called *in rem* (latin for "thing").

Second, jurisdiction can refer to the *subject matter* of the cases a court may hear. Within a county, the court system may be divided into juvenile court, small claims court, tax court, family court and courts of general jurisdiction empowered to hear civil and criminal cases of all sorts. The federal court system also has its specialized courts, but doesn't have nearly as many divisions according to subject matter. The best known special divisions in the federal system are the U.S. Bankruptcy and U.S. Tax courts.

Third, jurisdiction is also defined by whether or not a court has *original* jurisdiction or hears a case only on appeal *(appellate jurisdiction)*. A court that hears a case first is said to be a trial court: it hears the facts. Its conclusions—whether by a judge or a jury—about the facts of a case are final; whatever is decided to be the true set of facts about the original incident are the only facts that can be considered in an appeal.

Appeals. Appeals only concern mistakes of law, because, under the U.S. Constitution, only a trial court can determine the facts. This means that a court that hears a case on appeal can review only how the previous judge applied the law in the case; it cannot conclude that the facts determined earlier are incorrect. It can conclude, however, that the process of determining those facts was incorrect and order a new trial.

Take, for example, a situation involving a state employee who is discriminated against on the job. The trial court refuses to apply federal civil rights laws on the grounds that the employee works for the state, and thus only state civil rights laws are applicable. A legitimate appeal might be based on the claim that the federal laws apply even to disputes involving employees of a state government. An appeals judge could rule that the trial court committed an error of law. A new trial would be ordered and the proper laws would be applied.

Not all appeals result in new trials, however. Most either uphold the lower court's decision or overturn it. In either case, the appellate court may issue its own reasoning.

It is important to understand that appeals courts make decisions only about the rules by which trial judges apply the law to specific cases. These rules, as discussed above, make up the common law. This is why appellate court decisions are the ones recorded in case-law books. The whole point of collecting thousands of cases in print is that it slowly helps build a set of rules for the application of the law within a given jurisdiction. Trial court cases are usually not reported unless they lead to a decision that somehow modifies or clarifies an essential point about the rules of law.

Most cases start at the lowest trial level in the applicable court system. The party that loses (or doesn't win enough) can then appeal to an intermediate appeals court on the grounds that an error was made in the application of the law. Review by this appellate court (in most states called the *Court of Appeals*), can then be appealed by either party to the highest level appellate court (usually called the state's *Supreme Court*). Some states have only two levels of courts. See HALT's *Citizens Legal Manual,* **Courts & Judges,** for a description of each state's court system.

Understanding jurisdiction will help you focus your research on the court (or courts) that may have made important decisions about questions similar to yours. From the thousands of case-law books you encounter, you can immediately narrow your search to a few once you have decided which court has jurisdiction. Both jurisdiction and other aspects of case law research are discussed in greater detail in Chapter 12.

CHAPTER 5

Defining the Problem

Legal research is mostly a language game. Finding the right words to describe your particular problem is the first step—and it is often the most important one. As in any other specialized field, words have precise meanings. What makes the law especially tricky is that, unlike science or engineering where technical words are readily identifiable as specialized terms, the law often gives common words highly specialized meanings.

For example, you might comment on the large number of house break-ins in your area by saying, "We've had a lot of robberies recently." To someone familiar with the law, the word "robbery" refers only to theft from a person, not from a house. Theft by breaking into a house is a "burglary." A person familiar with the law would understand your comment as something other than what you intended.

Fortunately, you don't have to know all the correct definitions to start your legal research. As you progress in answering your question, you can clarify your understanding of the legal terms involved and learn to recognize the more technical terms used to describe situations similar to yours. The remainder of this chapter will show you how to build a list of words and questions that can be used to help you properly define your research problem.

CREATE A WORD LIST

Get started with your research by creating a word list that describes your situation. This list will serve as the initial point of reference in your research. It will be expanded and revised as you narrow your research and begin to discover answers to your questions.

West Publishing recommends the TARP system for generating word lists:

Things—such as deeds, property, contracts, injury, employment, automobiles, wills, taxes, animals, destruction, etc.

Actions—such as negligence, trespass, malpractice, fraud, breach of contract, assault, nuisance, divorce, etc.

Remedies—such as damages, restitution, injunctions or court orders for specific performance, etc.

Parties—those involved, such as minors, businesses, corporations, decedents, tenants, landlords, retailers or members of a class (such as women, minorities, the elderly, taxpayers, etc.).

To use the TARP system, list key words from your legal situation that fit into some or all of the TARP categories. Probably the easiest to generate will be in the T and P groups.

The following examples demonstrate the way in which the TARP system can help you create word lists:

• A neighbor's tree hangs over your yard and shades your garden. You want to find out if you have the right to prune the offending branches. The TARP words that you would generate are: *Things*—trees, adjoining property; *Action*—nuisance; *Parties*—landowners, neighbors; *Remedies*—court order for specific performance. With these few words, believe it or not, you are well on your way to solving your research problem.

• You suspect that the personal representative of your aunt's estate is mismanaging the assets. You want to learn about the procedure and the grounds for removing a personal representative. The T and P words: estate and personal representative. The Action: misappropriation. The Remedy: removal.

• While you're mowing the lawn, a jogger's dog jumps over your fence and bites your leg. You want to find out if you can be reimbursed for your medical expenses and trauma. The T and P words: dogs and dog bites. The A words: trespass and battery, for example. The R words: damages and animal control sanctions.

• You hire a plumber to install a new hot water heater. The plumber botches the job, leaving you with a flooded basement. You want the plumber to refund his fee and pay for the water damage. The T and P words: contracts, home repair, destruction and contractor. Actions: breach of contract and negligence. Remedies: damages and restitution.

Another important tool in generating word lists is a standard law dictionary or a plain-language dictionary. If, for example, you want to find out about probate in your state and know very little about the subject, a law dictionary can suggest many terms that will broaden the topic for you. A look in *Black's Law Dictionary* under "Probate" and related terms yields the following words and phrases:

administrator
court of probate

deceased person
decedent
executor
guardian
last will and testament
probate bond
probate code

Any of the above terms will in turn lead to others. For example, the definition of "probate jurisdiction" includes such helpful phrases as "establishment of wills," "settlement of decedents' estates," "supervision of guardianship of infants," "control of infants' property" and "allotment of dower." Each of these leads to important categories that should be investigated if you want an overall understanding of probate law in your state. This list can also help narrow your search if what you want is to probe only one or two select areas.

FORMULATE YOUR LEGAL QUESTIONS

Now that you have created word lists based on the TARP system and some help from a dictionary, consider some of the specific issues involved in your legal question. Formulate the questions you need answered.

Returning to the dog biting example above, you might break down your search into some specific, answerable questions, such as:

- Who is responsible for an injury caused by a biting dog?
- What facts do I have to prove to sue and win compensation for the dog bite?
- Is there a statute or ordinance that covers dog bites?
- Does it make a difference if the dog has or has not ever bitten anyone before?

Keep in mind that your questions may change as your research progresses. In this example, you may start out thinking that your issue involves dogs, only to find out that it is really involves the duties of a landowner to prevent harm from dangerous conditions on the land.

CATEGORIZE YOUR RESEARCH

Once you have formed word lists and questions, you will need to classify your legal issue. Based on your word lists, answer the following three questions:

- Does it involve federal law, state law or both? (Most legal issues involve state rather than federal law.)
- Does it involve criminal law or civil law?
- Does it involve the substance of the law or a legal procedure?

Continuing with the dog biting example above, the issue pertains to city, county and state law. This could be both a civil and criminal matter, depending on the state laws. The legal issues are substantive, rather than procedural. Now that you have answered these questions, you will find it much easier to choose useful background resources.

FIND APPROPRIATE BACKGROUND RESOURCES

Reading through a self-help book about the general area of law governing your issue will help you frame your research into your specific legal question and will help you understand the answers you find. Nolo publishes a number of plain language guides on numerous legal topics and much of the material is free and available on Nolo's Web site, *www.nolo.com*. In addition, HALT has published a number of inexpensive books on various legal topics and distributes free pamphlets and loose-leaf materials on many issues.

You can also turn to law school materials, including books published by West Publishing, such as the Nutshell and Black Letter Law series. The West Publishing Web site, *west.thomson.com/store/completelistTopics.asp*, offers numerous materials on a wide range of topics, from bankruptcy to landlord-tenant to real estate issues. From there, you can select from books, CD-ROMs, tapes and loose-leaf materials specific to your legal problem. Some of these materials contain complicated legal jargon, but most contain glossaries that explain terms in plain-language.

LOOK FOR STATUTES AND CASES

After you review background resources, you will want to proceed to the law itself. You should start by hunting for statutes and rules and then find court decisions that interpret them. However, some important areas of the law are developed primarily in the courts—the law of torts (or personal injuries) is a good example. If you have a tort problem, you might wish to start with cases first and then research statutory law if and when it is indicated.

You can find a number of free online resources, such as *Findlaw.com*, which will allow you to plug in search terms based on your word lists and find appropriate law. In addition, you can show your word list to a law librarian, who can direct you to books in the library that may help you find the answer to your legal questions.

Now that you know how to define your legal issue, you can use the remaining chapters of this book to learn how to use the library's resources to find relevant statutes and court decisions.

CHAPTER 6

Secondary Research

Now that you have a framework (your key words and questions), the next step is to educate yourself about the general topic you are studying. This will add to your vocabulary and help make sure you haven't missed any important issues.

Several sources offer both general information about the law and specific references to cases and statutes that may be central to your research. All of these secondary sources will, at the very least, provide an overview that will get you started and may even answer your questions.

It's always a good idea to start your research with secondary sources and, in particular, with those sources that are easiest for legal consumers to use and understand. If your question is not complex or unique, you will probably be able to find your answer here. These sources contain easy-to-read text that cuts through much of the extraneous material found in other sources like cases and statutes. Many secondary sources will, however, refer you to those materials so you will have the actual primary source to use as justification for your findings in court papers.

Regardless of the secondary sources you decide to use, you should follow these few rules:

1. Unless your legal question is very straightforward, never rely entirely on information in a secondary source (especially if you're involved in litigation). The source is someone's interpretation of the law. You should usually double-check the primary source and be sure that you understand it, too.

2. While it's preferable to cite original sources, referencing authoritative treaties and restatements of the law is a generally accepted practice.

3. Always check the *pocket part* of your source. These are updates published annually or more often and can be found in the back, in a special

pocket on the book's binding. (Sometimes, if the pocket part gets too large to fit in the book, it will be printed as a supplement, which is shelved next to the book.) Checking this will ensure that you are reading the most recent materials and that the law hasn't changed. This is critical: old law is bad law.

LEGAL PUBLISHERS

Before describing the various secondary resources available, it is helpful to understand a bit about legal publishing. There are many publishers of legal information, but by and large, there are two major ones that you will repeatedly run into during your research—West and LexisNexis. Each owns and promotes its own network of primary and secondary sources. In some situations, one publisher or the other may be the sole source of the type of information you're looking for, while in other situations they will have competing products. This is important to remember for two reasons: first, you'll find references within each source to other resources owned by that company, and second, if you're not finding an answer in one source, check the other's product or a similar resource published by a different company to see if it covers the topic and provides any additional information.

This is not to say that LexisNexis and West are the only publishers you will find on the shelves, but they are the biggest publishers of U.S. legal information. You'll see others, including Aspen, Commerce Clearing House and Bureau of National Affairs.

In larger law libraries, you can usually find publishers of self-help legal materials represented as well. Many of these titles are set aside in special "law for the layperson" sections. A listing of some of the better self-help publishers is found in Appendix VI. Nolo is the premiere publisher of self-help legal materials. A visit to their Web site—*www.nolo.com*—is a must for serious do-it-yourselfers.

BOOKS

We begin first with a discussion of secondary sources that are easiest for nonlawyers to use and understand. These materials are particularly well-suited for those with simple legal research questions.

See Chapter 7 (Online Tools) for a quick overview about finding secondary sources through the Internet.

Popular Law Books (& other materials). Books, kits and software programs about the law written for nonlawyers have created a fast-growing industry. And for good reason. People want access to legal information that is accurate, understandable and affordable. More and more consumers are finding that their simple legal questions or concerns are answered through do-it-yourself materials found not only in larger law libraries, but also in bookstores, public libraries and online. For more information on the kinds of subjects covered by self-help legal publishers, check HALT's *Citizens Legal Manual,* **Do-It-Yourself Law: HALT's Guide to Self-Help Books, Kits & Software.**

Let's say, for example, you have a question about whether an adopted child is considered to be the same as a natural child—as an heir—within the meaning of the state intestacy law (the law that defines who receives from the estate of someone who dies without leaving a will). In many secondary sources (including those found in the popular law book section), you will be able to find listings in the index for terms such as "Intestacy," "Distribution to Heirs" and "Children." One or more of these terms will lead you to a discussion of whether adopted children are covered by statute.

A Californian who wants to find out more about the legal inheritance rights of his adopted children doesn't even need to step into a law library to get an answer. He can find it in Nolo's *How to Probate an Estate (in California).* It addresses not only inheritance issues for adopted children but for all children—even those born out of wedlock. The book provides a general but thorough explanation of what the state's probate code says about adopted children and then refers you on to the specific cite in the California Probate Code that addresses all parent-and-child relationships.

Nolo even has a title on adopting stepchildren should our hypothetical Californian want to add to his family. The point here is that self-help legal materials (books, kits and software programs) have come a long way in the past decade. They provide consumers with a wealth of information on the law and often provide the forms necessary to complete simple but important legal transactions. A fuller discussion about using form books, kits and software to handle your own legal work can be found in the next chapter.

The downside of these books is that if your problem is particularly complicated, they may not go into enough depth for you. However, they may give you an indication of the next resource that would be helpful to use.

Nutshell and Black Letter Series. You might call these "Cliffs Notes" for law students. These plain-language study guides are published by West. Each is designed to help a law student recognize and understand the basic principles and issues of law covered in a law school course. They run about 300 pages long and include an index. Written by experienced law school teachers who are recognized authorities on the subject, these books can provide a quick and accurate lesson on both civil and criminal legal topics. Some examples include: *Administrative Law, Constitutional Law, Workers Compensation and Employee Protection Laws, Landlord and Tenant Law* and *Sex Discrimination.*

Treatises and Hornbooks. A *treatise* is a fancy term for a book written by a legal expert about a body of law, such as contracts, civil procedure, wills and trusts and so forth. A treatise may be a single volume or run to several volumes and can be found in loose-leaf or bound form. They are often updated by new releases (in the case of loose-leafs) or supplements or pocket parts (for bound treatises) or by a new edition of the book. *Hornbooks* are a subset of treatises, written for law students. Treatises—particularly the introductory texts—can be helpful in explaining general as well as complicated concepts of law.

The overview nature of introductory treatises can help you identify your legal problem. These books are written like text books and will use footnotes to refer you to cases, statutes and other sources. Investigate these primary sources for more information. Once you have a handle on your issue, you might check more detailed treatises that go into great depth on particular points of law.

Finding Books. To locate these texts, look in the law library's catalog. Almost all catalogs in every type of library are online and are available to library users. In fact, you've probably had experience using such a catalog at some time in your life. Many of these are even accessible through the Internet on the library's homepage. These catalogs (sometimes called OPACs, short for Online Public Access Catalogs) look different from library to library, but they all tend to work in basically the same ways. You can search by author, title, keyword, subject or some combination of these.

If you don't know the author or title of a book on your topic, the best choice is to perform a keyword or subject search using your word list that you've been working with all along. If you don't find any books on your topic, it may be that your search is too narrow. If you're interested in finding out how to remove an executor from your uncle's will, instead of searching for "removal of executors in Texas", try something like "estates and Texas," which may lead you to a book that has a chapter or a few paragraphs devoted to the grounds for an executor's removal in that state.

If you're having trouble using the library's catalog, look for a help button or link that will provide you with instructions and examples. If this doesn't help, ask a librarian to get you going in the right direction.

Once you've found a search that works, the OPAC will return a list of books for you to choose from. The record for each book will include a brief description along with subject headings that apply to the book, such as

"Negligence—United States." In online catalogs, these subjects are often clickable and will give you a list of all of the books in the library that also fall under that subject. In this way, once you've found a book or two on your topic, you can quickly find several more.

The other important piece of information you'll find in each book's record is the call number, which tells you how to find the book on the shelf. Write this down for any book you want to look at, along with the title, the date and the author. After you complete a list of a few books, start collecting them.

Books in a library are grouped by subject matter. Be sure to look at the books next to and in the same general area as any book chosen using the catalog, as this is often an excellent way to find books that didn't turn up in your catalog search.

LEGAL ENCYCLOPEDIAS

Legal encyclopedias provide general information about various types of law, legal concepts and special topics. Most include cross-references and bibliographies that can lead you directly to the answers and the primary sources you need.

A popular legal encyclopedia for do-it-yourselfers is Nolo's *Quicken Lawyer Personal* which is primarily an estate-planning software program. However, it also offers information and forms on lots of other legal topics, such as childcare, general bill of sales and simple authorization forms. If your law library's "law for the layperson" section doesn't carry it or some of the other self-help legal encyclopedias, check a local bookstore or search online.

More traditional legal encyclopedias include the *Corpus Juris Secundum (C.J.S.)* and *American Jurisprudence, Second Series (Am. Jur. 2d)*, both owned by West. Until the late 1990s, however, *Am. Jur. 2d* was owned by LexisNexis, and some volumes still contain references to that publisher's products.

Even though both encyclopedias are now under one publisher's roof, in general, the materials in *Am. Jur. 2d.* tend to be more readable and useful for nonlawyers. *C.J.S.* and related products may be more comprehensive, but they tend to lead the researcher straight to case law, which is rarely the best way to approach a legal problem.

Unfortunately, unless you have access to a law school or a fairly large law library, you won't be able to choose between the two encyclopedias. Libraries with limited budgets usually purchase one or the other but not both. For that reason, instructions for using both sets of encyclopedias are given below. If you have a choice between them, don't feel like you have to look up every aspect of your problem in both sets. Try each set out and decide which you like better.

CORPUS JURIS SECUNDUM (C.J.S.)

1. Start with the "General Index" located at the end of the set. By using your word list, you should be able to locate sections of the encyclopedia that deal with your legal questions. The "General Index" will lead you to the appropriate title abbreviation (a list of titles and their abbreviations is located at the beginning of the index), section numbers (marked §) and page numbers. Use the "General Index" of the *C.J.S.* to modify and expand your word lists. Be sure to write down all references to related topics.

2. The *C.J.S.* volumes are arranged alphabetically by subject, and the contents of each volume are arranged by section number. Look at the outlines in the front of each volume of the encyclopedia that you are referred to. Do this before you begin reading the sections and pages that were indicated by the "General Index." An *"Analysis"* outline will direct you to the sections in the volume that are related to your topic. The *"Sub-analysis"* outline provides the same information as the *"Analysis"* outline, but in greater detail. A reading of this second outline will give you a broad overview of all the topics included in this area of the law. The two outlines together will help you find related topics that may be of interest.

3. Each volume of the *C.J.S.* contains an index that refers only to sections in that volume. By using the "General Index" to get you to the correct volume, and the volume's index to discover additional research leads, you will quickly learn to pull the relevant background material out of the mass of information in the encyclopedia. In the beginning, however, err on the side of including too much rather than risk overlooking a section or reference that could prove crucial to understanding your research topic.

4. Turn to the numbered sections. These offer a general discussion and footnotes citing particular cases and other sections of *C.J.S.* Each of these sections is preceded by research notes that direct you to other sections in the *C.J.S.* and by library references that refer to other secondary sources and indicate the section's topic and key number (these will look like "Negligence 35" and will include a picture of a small key before the number). These topics and key numbers make up the crux of the West case-finding system, and are covered in more detail in Chapter 14. Although of little use at this stage of your research, make a note of the topic and key number associated with sections that are of particular interest to you as you discover them.

5. A table of all of the federal laws and rules as well as a multi-volume listing of all of the cases mentioned in the *C.J.S.* can be found at the end of the set. The tables provide cross-references to the topics and sections of the encyclopedia where these laws and cases are cited.

6. Before leaving a volume of the *C.J.S.*, be sure to check the pocket parts and note each pocket's date. If it's not recent, you may want to be particularly careful to *shepardize* (update) the cases and statues cited in both the encyclopedia and the pocket part in a state or federal Shepard's citator when you reach that stage of the research process. *(See Chapter 15.)*

AMERICAN JURISPRUDENCE (AM. JUR. 2D)

The encyclopedia *American Jurisprudence, Second Series (Am. Jur. 2d)* has information that is similar to the *C.J.S.*, but it is organized differently. The volumes on the shelves may be more recent than comparable volumes of the *C.J.S.*, though as long as the pocket parts are current, the actual age of the volume doesn't matter. If you have a choice between the two encyclopedias, check the publishing dates of the volumes that cover your topic before deciding which one to use.

1. As with the *C.J.S.*, start with the "General Index," then turn to the index at the back of each title volume. Again like the *C.J.S.*, the *Am. Jur. 2d* has *"Analysis"* and *"Sub-analysis"* outlines at the beginning of each volume. To find what you need, simply follow the procedure in steps (1) through (5) in the *C.J.S.* section above. Note that since becoming a West product, *Am. Jur. 2d.* now includes West's topics and key numbers in its updated volumes and pocket parts published after that point.

2. One special feature of the *Am. Jur. 2d* is that its sections include extensive cross-references to the *American Law Reports (A.L.R.) (discussed below)* as well as law-review articles and practice aids *(also discussed below and in Chapter 8).*

3. Another feature is the volume of *New Topic Service,* which gives up-to-date references to new topics in the encyclopedia. New developments in the law are often rooted in older trends, and the relationship is not always obvious—especially to nonlawyers. *The New Topic Service* helps you research new areas of the law by indicating their connections to key words, phrases and concepts.

4. As with the *C.J.S.*, if you are dealing with a statute and know its title and section number, you can use the *Table of Statutes and Rules Cited* to cross-reference directly to the appropriate *Am. Jur. 2d* titles and sections. All statutes and administrative rules cited within *Am. Jur. 2d* are included in the *Table of Statutes and Rules Cited* located with the index. Similar tables are found within each *Am. Jur. 2d* topic, but they refer you only to statutes covered within that topic. All of these tables include only federal statutes, federal rules of procedure and evidence and uniform laws (Uniform Commercial Code, Uniform Probate Code, etc.). If you want to trace applications of a state statute, these tables will not help you.

5. Also as with the *C.J.S.*, be sure to check volume supplements and pocket parts to update your information. You can then shepardize to learn any recent changes. *(See Chapter 15.)*

STATE ENCYCLOPEDIAS

Some legal encyclopedias cover only the laws of a particular state. If you know that you are dealing with a question of state law, a state encyclopedia will give you specific answers about your state's laws. This is far superior to the general statement of law usually found in national encyclopedias.

If published by LexisNexis or West (as most are), a state's encyclopedia may follow the format of *C.J.S.* or *Am. Jur. 2d*. Expect the same sorts of information, including cross-references and citations to statutes and cases. The major difference will be that the state encyclopedia focuses exclusively on the law of that state.

AMERICAN LAW REPORTS (A.L.R.)

Lawyers Co-operative's *A.L.R.* system is a cross between a case reporter and a law journal. Each volume contains a handful of appellate cases annotated by lengthy articles (called annotations in *A.L.R.*). Each annotation evaluates all of the case law on the specific point of law considered in one of the appellate cases. There are thousands of such annotations in *A.L.R.* Many researchers turn to this set for background information before they look at case or statutory law. Keep in mind that, although there are plenty of articles, the fact that they are so specific can mean that your topic may not be covered or may only be briefly touched on. Still, because of the depth of information that can be found in an annotation, the *A.L.R.* is certainly worth your time to explore.

The *A.L.R.* system contains six series: the *A.L.R. 1st* covers state and federal cases reported between 1919 and 1948; *A.L.R. 2nd* continues these from 1948 to 1965; *A.L.R. 3rd* includes state and federal topics from 1965 to 1969 and only state topics from 1969 to 1980; *A.L.R. 4th* covers 1980 to 1991; and the *5th* series continues to the present. *A.L.R. Federal* includes all federal cases and topics beginning in 1969.

The annotations, which make up the heart of the set, precede the reported cases. They begin with an outline of how the issues in the annotation are organized. "Related Research References" are listed after this outline, and may include such items as references to encyclopedias, practice aids, law review articles and primary materials such as statutes. In newer volumes, you may also find topics and key numbers listed under the heading "West Digest Key Numbers." Next, an index shows where key terms are discussed in the annotation. A *Jurisdictional Table of Cited Statutes and Cases* (or something similarly-named) indicates whether a case or statute from your jurisdiction is discussed in the annotation. In the *A.L.R. Federal* series, this information is broken into two tables called "Statutory Text" which reprints the pertinent statutory sections, and "Table of Cases."

The text of the annotation begins with a "Scope" section that briefly describes the contents. The next section, "Related Annotations," cites other *A.L.R.* annotations that discuss related legal topics. The "Summary" gives an overview of the law that relates to the topic and the "Practice Pointers" indicate how the law can be applied. The remainder of the text is the annotation itself—an in-depth analysis of the case law on the topic. References to other legal-reference sources, especially cases, are given throughout.

Locating and Updating A.L.R. Annotations. Unlike an encyclopedia, annotations are not arranged by subject. Instead, they are printed chronologically as they are written, which makes it unpractical and infeasible to browse them as you would *C.J.S.* or *Am. Jur. 2d.*

You can locate annotations in the *A.L.R.* in several ways, however. You may, of course, be referred directly to a particular annotation by a legal encyclopedia, treatise or other work. If not, the easiest approach is to use one of the *A.L.R.* quick indexes, which index the annotations by subject matter. The best one to begin with (unless your topic is a federal issue) is the red, soft cover "*A.L.R. Quick Index*," located at the end of the set. This index covers *A.L.R. 3rd, 4th,* and *5th* only and, for most purposes, is sufficient for getting you into some relevant annotations, which in turn will refer you to others. There are also quick indexes that cover only one series. For instance, the "*A.L.R. 1st Quick Index*" covers the *A.L.R.1st*. The "*A.L.R. Federal Quick Index*" indexes all of the federal topics.

There is also a full index which covers the whole *A.L.R.* with the exception of the *1st* series. Use this index if you can't find an annotation on your topic through a quick index.

Whenever you are referred to an *A.L.R.* annotation, always consult the "Annotation History Table" first. Found in a separate volume of tables at the end of the full index and its pocket part, this will tell you if an annotation has been supplemented or superseded by a later annotation. Changes in the law make it sometimes necessary to replace an annotation on a topic, rendering the earlier version obsolete. Because the volumes are not republished, however, superseded annotations are never removed, even though they should never be relied upon.

Once you have selected your annotation and determined that it is still an accurate reflection of the law, be sure to check the pocket part in the back of the volume you're using. It will contain additions to the text as well as new cases and other sources of law.

LAW JOURNAL ARTICLES

Law journals (also called law reviews) are journals published by law schools and legal associations. They contain anywhere from a few to many articles in each issue. New issues are usually available three or four times a year. Law journals can be either general or topical in scope. For example, a general law review's coverage might be compared to that of *Time* magazine, where any current news story may be featured. On the other hand, a topical journal is more like *Scientific American,* where one would expect to find articles dealing with various aspects of just one subject.

The articles are usually written by law professors or selected law students who have spent a great deal of time researching a particular area of the law. They often contain in-depth analysis that may be related to your problem. Law journal articles also can be general surveys of an area of law or they can be highly detailed analyses of certain court cases and related statutes, like an *A.L.R.* annotation. Either way, reading such articles may prove helpful. Most are based on exhaustive research and the extensive footnotes may lead you to any number of primary and secondary sources.

Journals are not browsable like an encyclopedia. Like the *A.L.R.,* journal articles are published chronologically and not by topic. Even in a topical journal, the articles don't follow an orderly arrangement. To find articles, you'll need to find citations to them, either from other resources already discussed or through an index.

There are two indexes devoted to law journals, both of which are available online, if the library subscribes to them. The first of these is called *LegalTrac,* and the other is *Index to Legal Periodicals (ILP)*. While at first glance these appear very different from each other, they both can be searched in the same way: by author, title, subject, keyword or a combination of these. Both cover articles ranging back to about 1980. The main difference between the two is that *LegalTrac* indexes about 900 law and bar association journals (bar journals contain much shorter, practical articles that usually lack extensive footnotes), while *ILP* indexes about 600 journals, and omits bar journals. Also, *LegalTrac* is updated every day, and *ILP* is updated about once a month.

Your search results from either index will give you citation information which you can then use to look at the articles in print. Rarely will an article appear in full-text in one of the indexes. Both indexes have "Help" screens in case you have trouble searching them. It is not a bad idea to glance at the "Help" screens anyway, to make sure you're searching in the best way possible.

If the library does not subscribe to either index online, look for the print versions of either of them. The disadvantage to using the print sets is that they don't cumulate; that is, you must look up your topic in each year's volume as far back as you care to find articles. If you sought articles on, say, negligence from 2000 to present, you would need to look in the 2000 volume, the 2001 volume, and so on, up to the latest volume available (or, more likely, you'd start with the current volume and work backwards until you found something). Also, the print indexes are not as current as their online counterparts.

LegalTrac's print component is the *Legal Resources Index,* and it covers journals from 1980 to the present. *ILP's* print counterpart is also called the *Index to Legal Periodicals,* and it covers journals from as far back as the late 1700's through the present. These sets are usually kept in the reference or periodicals sections of the library.

Small law libraries may not have any version of a law journal index simply because they don't subscribe to enough journals to need them. If this is the case, your best bet is to check the nearest public or university library to see if they subscribe to an index (online or in print) that includes some law journals. (General indexes, such as *InfoTrac,* do.) If you can find even a citation or two for journal articles to take with you to the law library, you'll find cites to other articles within the articles you gleaned from the index.

LOOSE-LEAF SERVICES

Loose-leaf services are regularly updated reports that combine subject-related case law, statutory law and regulatory law as well as editor-written commentary, making this a source of both primary and secondary law. They are actually a form of reporter that is organized by subject matter rather than jurisdiction. They get their name from the fact that they are large loose-leaf binders into which the latest update can be inserted. Updates are usually published weekly, bi-weekly or monthly.

Loose-leafs are important research tools largely because of the huge amount of regulatory law from administrative agencies. Their editors review all of the decisions of those bodies that have an impact on a given area of law and report these decisions in one place. A list of loose-leaf services is included in Appendix III.

Be cautioned: loose-leafs are complete but complicated to use. They have many different sections and are notorious for having a confusing system of page numbering with an endless number of sections (§§), paragraphs (¶) and decimals. If you decide to use a loose-leaf service, be sure to read its section on "How to Use this Book" before you begin. The instructions will identify the parts of the service in which you should look for your answers.

CHAPTER 7

Online Tools

ONLINE LEGAL RESEARCH – AN OVERVIEW

One of the most far-reaching developments in legal research in the past few years is the ability to find a tremendous amount of information online, oftentimes for free. Cases, statutes, regulations and other legal resources, once found only in books or at the courthouse, are now posted on the Internet by governments, non-profit groups and anyone else with an interest in the law.

This means that you can do a lot of research legwork from somewhere besides a law library, such as from your home or a public library. There are several things to note about online research, however. First of all, and probably most importantly, keep in mind that you usually get what you pay for. In other words, free sites normally give you the basics, but none of the finding aids or commentary to help your research along. Other times, they'll give you some introductory information, but to get more than that, you'll be asked for a credit card number. When you do find information, it is usually stripped of any editorial comment, West key numbers or other added features.

Also, information found online, especially free information, must be examined carefully to make sure it's current, accurate and reliable. Pay attention to the source where you found something. Is it from a government or university site? The court or the legislature itself? Or can you even tell who is providing the information? Trust your instincts. If the Web site looks shoddy and ill-maintained, chances are the information contained within may be out-of-date or error-ridden. To be safe, try to find the same case or statute in a book or at a more reputable site.

Sites that charge for information sometimes can be more reliable if they have a company reputation to worry about. However, this is not always the case and the same sorts of issues apply as for free sites. The bottom line is to approach any online resource with open eyes and make sure that it's a good value for your dollar, if you choose to pay for something.

Another thing to keep in mind when researching online is that you will probably be able to find free sources of primary materials—cases, statutes and the like—without too much difficulty. Some forms and court rules are also fairly easy to come by. The selection of free secondary materials online, on the other hand, is much smaller. Although the availability of materials online has added an entirely new dimension to the process of legal research, the basics are still the same. Start with secondary sources to get a feel for the law and perhaps answer your question. Then move into primary research. In many instances, that means that to start or fill in gaps in their research, most people will still need to use the books in the library. However, as the amount of online material grows, the need for books decreases.

The Web sites referred to in the rest of this chapter are by no means an exhaustive list of legal Web sites. Appendix II and VI have a fuller list of Web sites and other computer resources, but, of course, no list of Internet resources is ever completely up-to-date. We recommend you make use of search engines and online directories to find additional Web sites that may be relevant to your research.

SECONDARY RESOURCES

As with research in the library, you should start your research by trying to understand the lay of the land in the area of law relating to your situation. Unfortunately, many of the resources mentioned in the previous chapter—those that provide a general outline of the law in a particular field—are not available online. However, there are some Internet sources for this sort of general information.

Consumer-friendly Legal Web Sites. There are a growing number of sites that are geared toward nonlawyers using the legal system *(see Appendix II and VI)*. Sites such as *www.nolo.com* and *www.findlaw.com/public* are designed to help everyday people learn about the law. These types of sites can be used in two ways. First, there is usually a topical index, which you can browse to find information about the area of law in which you are interested. Second, you can often perform a keyword search by entering a few terms relevant to the area you are researching. Keyword searches and topical browsing are common to Internet legal research and can be found on many of the other types of sites mentioned below. These powerful tools are one of the ways in which Internet research can be more efficient than research in books.

Government Web Sites. These are often the best place to visit to find out about various legal and administrative procedures, as well as issues of law dealing with the government. Each state has a Web site with the address *www.state.XX.us* (where "XX" is the state's two letter postal abbreviation, in lower case letters). State Web sites generally have links to the state court system Web site, which will often tell you about procedures for filing a lawsuit or defending against one. Some state court Web sites also include extensive self-help law sections. The state Web site also usually has links to state consumer and regulatory agencies, which often have information on the areas of law they regulate. For federal issues, there are similar Web pages which you can link to through *www.firstgov.gov*.

Bar Association Web Sites. Many state bar associations contain information for nonlawyers on their Web sites. Such material can include information about how the legal system works in that state. These sites may also provide answers to frequently-asked legal questions and overviews of particular areas of law.

PRIMARY RESOURCES

Primary resources, such as court decisions and statutes, make up the bulk of legal information on the Web. As explained in the following chapter, these resources often deal with very specific situations and are only useful after you have obtained a general understanding of the law dealing with your issue.

Government Web Sites. Many state government Web sites include cases and statutes from that state. These are generally not searchable by concept, but some sites will present the entire state code by section, which allows some browsing. A state's case law is usually found on the judiciary section of its site; the statutes are usually found in the legislative site. Counties and cities may also have local ordinances on their Web sites. The Web sites for federal agencies and departments may have similar links to laws relevant to their missions.

General Legal Web Sites. A growing number of sites contain a large selection of primary materials. Sites such as Findlaw *(www.findlaw.com)* and Cornell University's Legal Information Institute *(www.law.cornell.edu)* contain federal and state codes and case law. They also may contain forms and articles that are helpful to you. The downside of such sites is that the information may not be searchable by keyword, which can be like having a table of contents for a book but no index. However, if you know the citation for a particular case or statute, chances are that you'll be able to find it on a Web site of this type.

Paid Legal Databases. These databases (Lexis and Westlaw are the two most popular) are the equivalent of having an entire law library at your fingertips. The downside is that they are extremely expensive. Appendix II describes these resources in more detail and provides some hints on how to use them without paying as much. However, unless you want to spend a lot of money or have a way to get free access to these databases, they may not be right for you.

CHAPTER 8

Practice Aids

Form books and their cousins, practice and procedure books, are the hands-on legal research tools lawyers use when drafting legal documents. They provide you sample forms and tips on procedures. They are collectively called practice aids.

If you're interested in drafting routine legal documents on your own or learning how to file a lawsuit against someone, we suggest—before launching into the practice aids offered through your local law library—that you check out many of the do-it-yourself legal forms, books and software programs now available. *(See Appendix VI.)*

Over the years, there has been a literal explosion in the number of high-quality products that let you take charge of your own legal affairs. The strengths and weaknesses of many of these products are profiled in HALT's *Citizens Legal Manual,* **Do-it-Yourself Law: HALT's Guide to Self-Help Books, Kits & Software.**

Some focus on a particular area of law, such as estate planning while others offer information and forms on a variety of legal subjects covering everything from real estate sales to borrowing and lending money to buying and selling goods. Some will take you, step-by-step, through the process of suing somebody—explaining when and how to initiate a lawsuit, compile evidence and cross examine witnesses. A good example is *Represent Yourself in Court: How to Prepare & Try a Winning Case,* by Nolo. It explains how to confidently handle a divorce, personal injury case, landlord-tenant dispute, breach of contract, small business dispute or any other civil lawsuit.

If you decide to use do-it-yourself legal materials to draft a legal document, you'll find that most products use one of two basic approaches. Some products provide a general library of legal information, standardized forms and instructions on how to complete them. Others use interactive computer programs that ask you a series of questions and then produce completed forms based on your answers.

An example of the latter is *Quicken WillMaker Plus 2004*—a HALT *Do-it-Yourself Best Buy.* This software program, which primarily covers estate-planning topics like will-writing, durable powers of attorney and living trusts, provides more than 30,000 document possibilities from a total of 46 different legal forms. It's simple to install, easy-to-use and offers extensive help both online and through a hard copy user's manual. In the end, you can produce a professional looking (and more importantly) accurate legal document that's state specific and tailored to your needs.

If you're not computer savvy (or don't have access to a computer), you can still turn to a variety of excellent do-it-yourself legal books and form kits. For a complete list of these titles, check HALT's book, **Do-it-Yourself Law.**

Many lawyers are undoubtedly using these products in their own practices. Of course, they also use the traditional kinds of practice guides discussed in this chapter. For more information on those guides, read on.

FORM BOOKS

Form books are collections of sample forms used in regular legal transactions, such as standard contracts, power-of-attorney agreements, releases, corporate forms and so on. Also called formularies, they are available in two types: general (for all aspects of legal practice) and subject-related (for a single topic or area of law). Form books for your state may also exist.

The general ones come in single and multi-volume editions. The larger ones are annotated, with each form cross-referenced to cases that have defined the meaning of each provision in the form. Forms themselves can be divided into those that deal with court procedure (such as filing a complaint or other processes of bringing and defending a case) and those that are concerned with substantive (actual) issues (such as a personal property lease). The main general sets of forms are: *American Jurisprudence Legal Forms Annotated, West's Legal Forms, Nichols Cyclopedia of Legal Forms Annotated,* and *American Jurisprudence Pleading and Practice Forms* (which tends to be heavily procedural). In addition, there are sets of procedural forms that focus solely on the federal-court system: *Federal Procedural Forms* and *West's Federal Forms.*

Subject-related form books have a greater variety of forms than a general book. They cover topics from criminal defense practice forms to standard forms for banking, real estate, divorce, will-drafting, bankruptcy procedures and so forth. If these are not in a collection of form books, they can be located using the library's catalog—search using the name of your topic and adding "and forms."

Many form books offer detailed checklists of what to include in a will, a sales contract or other documents. For example, the beginning of each volume of the *American Jurisprudence Legal Forms Annotated* contains checklists of items to consider when drafting a form.

Forms can be found in other types of resources, as well. You may run across them in treatises, the *Martindale-Hubbell Law Digest,* courts' rule books, other practice aids and even continuing legal education publications. Paralegal and legal secretaries' manuals also provide forms and show how to prepare them for presentation to a court.

A form book can give you an idea of the kinds of documents you can use to meet your legal needs, but they should be used carefully. Although they can suggest things you may want to include in your legal form, they should not be regarded as the established pattern for all such documents. Your situation may require special clauses that are not contained in a form contract or court motion. If you use form books, be sure you understand what the forms actually say before you apply them to your legal situation.

PRACTICE AND PROCEDURE BOOKS

Court Rules. With the exception of most small claims courts, all court systems have strict procedural rules. These are created by statutes and by rules of the U.S. Supreme Court (for federal courts) and each state's highest court (for state courts). The technical requirements for taking action in court are defined by these rules. They determine who is entitled to sue, the grounds for suing, the jurisdiction, the time limits, the papers required for filing and so on. Failure to follow these rules carefully can mean losing your case.

The rules that govern non-criminal matters are called the *Rules of Civil Procedure.* The federal laws that contain these rules for federal courts are located in Title 28 of the *United States Code (U.S.C.) (Judiciary and Judicial Procedures).* The *U.S.C.A. (United States Code Annotated)* and *U.S.C.S. (United States Code Service)* annotate these rules, and they also contain the procedural rules for several federal quasi-judicial forums as well. Special federal courts and many administrative agencies are covered in the Pike & Fischer *Administrative Law Service.* Finally, federal agencies (and some state agencies), often publish their procedural rules in a paperback edition that is sent free, upon request.

For additional information about federal rules, check a rules-practice set, such as *Federal Practice Procedure* (the Civil Procedure volumes are sometimes referred to as "Wright & Miller") or Moore's *Federal Practice.* These sources will give you a lot of information about each rule, and how to apply them in practice. Further, they will lead you to cases and other resources that interpret them.

State court rules are located in the state statutes under the topic of "Practice," "Civil Procedure," "Court Rules" or similar headings. They may also be shelved at the end of the state code in separate rule books. Federal District Courts and local state courts also issue their own rules about where papers should be filed, the forms that should be used and similar requirements. A set called *Federal Local Rules* contains these rules from federal courts. State local rules are sometimes available with the state rules. If not, ask the clerk of the court for a copy.

Many court rules are available for free online. See Appendix II for a list of such sites.

Other Practice Aids. There are three other practice aids which may be useful in your research. These are: *Causes of Action (COA), American Jurisprudence Trials (Am. Jur. Trials)* and *Am. Jur. Proof of Facts (PoF)*. Each of these sets provides very detailed articles that describe what you (or the other party) will need to prove in order to bring a case to court, how to prove a certain point to the judge or jury or how to conduct an aspect of a trial.

While this may sound far afield from the process of gathering information about your legal issue, the knowledge you can gain from these sets can be very useful. They provide forms, checklists, discussion and even sample testimony for specific situations. For example, in *Causes of Action,* you can find an article that guides you through a case against an employer for wrongful discharge of an employee. At its beginning, the article describes the available actions, the elements of the case, defenses, who can be sued and the types of damages that are usually recovered. The rest of the article is an in-depth discussion with citations to the laws of specific states. You can use this sort of practical information as a complement to your other research.

CHAPTER 9

State Statutes

Most legal questions involve state or federal statutes. This is because legislatures regularly try to solve problems by establishing rules about how competing interests should coexist. In addition, legislatures also often incorporate the decisions of the courts (the common law) into statutes.

For example, imagine that the courts in Illinois have decided over the years that the surviving spouse of someone who dies without a will should get half the property, with the remainder going to the children and parents. The legislature might eventually decide to pass a law that defines rules of distribution to heirs, either agreeing with the courts' rulings or establishing an alternative formula. If the formula is different, it might be contested in court and generate its own interpretive case law. Either way, it will be necessary to research *both* statutory law and case law to assure that you have the final, correct answer about how your spouse's estate must be divided.

It is usually best to begin this phase of research by looking at the state statutes. With any luck, one of the legal encyclopedias or another secondary source will have referred you to the statute that you need for further research. But, if they do not cover your topic, then you'll have to start with your key word list in the general index of your state's statutes. Start with federal statutes *(see Chapter 10)* only if you are sure your problem involves federal law (for example, the *Equal Opportunity Employment Act* or the *Americans with Disabilities Act)*.

Methods for locating applicable statutes are discussed here and in Chapter 10.

STATUTES AND CODES

Every state legislature meets and passes (or enacts) statutes during its general session. These laws are first published as *session laws* in the order in which they were passed. The first enacted law of a given year will be the first entry in that year's session law volume, the second will follow it and so on. Every state has a collection of these session laws.

Researching a statute in the session laws is nearly impossible, though, when you're looking for the laws on a particular topic. This is because the session laws are not arranged by subject. Furthermore, the collection of session laws will also contain laws that have been repealed, amended or are otherwise no longer in force as originally passed.

Fortunately, a system has evolved to fill the need to be able to find the current laws of a jurisdiction. At established intervals, usually at the end of one or more legislative sessions, most of a legislature's statutes or acts currently in force (usually excluding appropriations, authorizations and other budgetary laws) are collected and published, generally as Revised Statutes, Codes or Compilations. These terms have technical differences, but are commonly used interchangeably to mean a topical arrangement of all the laws currently in force in a jurisdiction. In this chapter, the word "code" is used to mean any such collection of state statutes. You should always use a code when you want to find the current statute(s) on your topic.

Your state will have at least one code and may have two or more. Codes come in two varieties: official and unofficial. Official codes (those that are so designated by statute or court rule) may take years to be published and be distributed to law libraries. Unofficial codes are produced much more quickly and are therefore more likely to be up-to-date than the most recent official codes.

Either type of code can be annotated or unannotated. Unannotated codes include only the actual wording of the statutes and minimal additional information, with no helpful interpretation, discussion or citations to other materials such as cases and law review articles. Annotated codes, on the other hand, include references to cases, law journals and other reference materials that can help explain the codified materials. These types of codes are typically produced by private publishers and may refer to other products owned by that company. For instance, codes put out by West will include topic and key numbers for use with the Digest System. *(See Chapter 14.)*

You should use the annotated statutes or code if it is available, but keep in mind that the annotations (including the case summaries) are *not* part of the law. You cannot refer to them as proof of anything. If it appears that one of the cases summarized in an annotation can help you, you must turn to and quote from the actual case—not the annotation. Of course, it is important to read these annotations and let them lead you to primary sources, such as case law, but don't rely on them as final statements of "the law."

The above may seem a little complex, but the important points to remember are: (1) if the name is used correctly, an "annotated code" contains more than just legislative acts; (2) a "code" is not the same as a constitution; and (3) primary sources that are "official" are not always the most helpful research tools—in fact, the opposite is usually true. This last point actually applies to most primary sources, not just codes.

THE ARRANGEMENT OF CODES

State statutes are published regularly and updated frequently. Your state's statutes will probably be available in any law library you visit in your state. All of the state statutes are organized similarly, but some states organize their statutes into titles (where each title deals with a different topic), while others (such as California) group their statutes into separate codes, such as a criminal code, a probate code, etc. These are still collectively referred to as the state code, however.

A page from the Iowa Code Annotated

§ 251.4   **CHILDREN AND FAMILIES**

251.4. Grants from state funds to counties

The state division may require as a condition of making available state assistance to counties for emergency relief purposes, that the county boards of supervisors shall establish budgets as needed in respect to the relief situation in the counties. — TEXT OF SECTION

Transferred from § 251.3 by the Code Editor for Code 1971. Amended by Acts 1981 (69 G.A.) ch. 117, § 1035; Acts 1983 (70 G.A.) ch. 123, §§ 101, 209. — SOURCE AND AMENDMENT INFORMATION

Historical and Statutory Notes

Derivation:

Acts 1967 (62 G.A.) ch. 209, § 424.
Codes 1966, 1962, 1958, 1954, 1950, 1946, 251.3.
Code 1939, § 3828.069.
Acts 1939 (48 G.A.) ch. 86, § 3.

The 1981 amendment rewrote the section, which prior thereto read:

"The state division shall have the authority to require as a condition of making available state assistance to counties for emergency relief purposes, that the county boards of supervisors shall make maximum tax levies for relief and establish such budgets as are needed in respect to the relief situation in the counties. The state division shall also have the authority to require as a condition of grants of state aid to the counties that the county board of supervisors shall make no transfers from the county poor

fund or charges against the county poor fund for purposes other than that for which the county poor fund is established by law, and it is hereby made mandatory upon the county board of supervisors, that taxes levied and collected for the county poor fund shall be expended only for the purposes levied."

The 1983 amendment rewrote the section, which prior thereto read:

"The state division may require as a condition of making available state assistance to counties for emergency relief purposes, that the county boards of supervisors shall make maximum tax levies for relief, establish budgets as needed in respect to the relief situation in the counties, and comply with restrictions in section 331.422, subsection 11."

Former § 251.4, Code 1966, was transferred to § 251.5 by the Code Editor for Code 1971. — HISTORICAL NOTES

Library References

Social Security and Public Welfare ⊜194.1. WESTLAW Topic No. 356A.

C.J.S. Social Security and Public Welfare § 115. — RELATED ENCYCLOPEDIA ARTICLE

Notes of Decisions

Conflict of interest   1

1. Conflict of interest
The offices of secretary of soldiers' relief commission and executive director of county poor

fund are compatible; hence, the holding of such offices by same person is not violation under this section. Op.Atty.Gen., Sept. 25, 1968 (No. 68-9-22). — RELATED CASES

The titles or codes may be further broken down into chapters. Each chapter deals with a subtopic of the title or code topic.

The text of the statutes are reproduced section-by-section in the code. Each section of a law is followed by some information about when it was passed, when it was amended (if applicable) and other historical information. If it is an annotated code, research references, such as case summaries and law journal citations, will come after the historical notes.

Each state code contains a table of contents and a detailed index. There is often an even more detailed index at the end of each title or topic. The code may contain other tables, such as a "Popular Name Table," which allows you to look up a law if you know its name. Codes are updated with pocket parts, supplements and, in many cases, with an "advance legislative service" (or something similarly named) that supplements the pocket parts with new laws from the current session of the legislature.

States use different citation formats when referring to their code. Some use something like §13.1-121, where 13.1 is the title and 121 is the section. Others may use a form such as Prob. C. §150, meaning Probate Code section 150. If it's not immediately obvious what the numbers and letters mean, see the forward or preface in any volume of the code to find out how to decipher them.

If you are not certain about the precise meaning of a word in a statute, look under "Definitions" in the index of the volume that contains the statute. Or you could look to see if there is a "Definitions" section at the beginning of the chapter where the section in question is found. The index will give you both the general location of all terms defined for a given chapter, and the specific location of important items. Always check the pocket part to see if any definitions have been amended to clarify particular points. If you cannot find a definition in the statutes, try *Black's Law Dictionary* or a plain-language dictionary.

USING STATE STATUTES

In general, researching statutes varies little from state to state. Even when looking up federal statutes, the process is largely the same. The steps are as follows:

1. Unless you have a citation to a statute from another source, begin with the index to the code using the terms you've used in other sources to find information.

2. Once you locate the correct code sections, find them in the main set of the code. If you don't understand the abbreviations used in the index, look in the front of the index for an abbreviation key.

3. Check for annotations that may give you cases, articles, forms and encyclopedia references and so on.

4. Be sure to check the pocket parts or supplementary materials at the end of the volume you're using and at the end of the code itself. *(More on this below.)*

For an in-depth example of how to research statutes, see the section entitled *An Example: Using an Index to Find Statutes* in Chapter 10.

POCKET PARTS AND ADVANCE LEGISLATIVE SERVICES

You have not finished researching statutes until you've checked the pocket part to see if the law has been revised recently. If you look at the back of any volume of the statutes, you will find the cumulative Annual Pocket Part for the most current year. This pamphlet includes all new laws and revisions passed in the most recent regular and special sessions of the state's legislature up through the date of the pocket part's publication.

The pocket part is arranged by articles and section numbers that correspond exactly to those in the statutes. If any section is modified by legislation or court rulings after the collected statutes or cases were printed, the pocket part prints the text of the new section or adds case notes or other annotations. An entire section reprinted in a pocket part completely replaces that section in the text of the statutes or code. If the section you are researching has not been changed or added to, you will find no references to that section in the pocket part.

Some states reprint a newly revised section in the pocket part with asterisks and underlining to show where the changes occur. ~~Struck through~~ text, three asterisks (***) or something similar indicate where words, phrases or sentences in the original statute have been omitted or are being deleted. Underlined, italicized, bolded or similarly-emphasized words and phrases are the new additions. For example, consider the sentence: "This act imposes liability upon specified persons of actual damages plus a $50 penalty, up to a total of $10,000, for failure to comply." In the pocket part, the revised sentence might appear as "This act imposes liability upon specified persons of actual damages plus a *** <u>$250 civil penalty</u> *** for failure to comply." You might also see it as "This act imposes liability upon specified persons of actual damages plus a ~~$50 penalty, up to a total of $10,000,~~ $250 civil penalty for failure to comply."

Always check the pocket part for every section that you read in the statutes. One minor legislative change or additional court case can greatly alter the meaning of an article or section. The importance of knowing the most current law when dealing with primary materials such as statutes cannot be overstated.

Pocket parts for codes are only printed once per year in most states. That means that your code may be as much as a year out-of-date when you use it. To bring your research up-to-date, use the advance legislative service that is found at the end of the code. These vary slightly from state to state, but they contain an index and some tables to help you find out if your code section has been updated. The best way to use them is to look up your code section in the table in the latest issue available. If your section is in there, it will tell you which session law affected it. The rest of the advance legislative service reprints these session laws in order of passage, so you can use the reference from the table to read the new law.

When a bill is enacted by a state legislature, some states will print it in slip form—that is, on individual sheets of paper. Libraries may collect these for whatever state the library is located in, but may not receive them for other states. Use the advance legislative service where possible to update the code beyond the pocket parts. Another good place to find these new laws is on the state's Web site, as many states publish them there as well.

To bring the pocket part or any other information about a statute completely up to date, you can always *shepardize* the material. To learn more about shepardizing, see Chapter 15.

LEGISLATIVE HISTORY

To understand how a statute should be interpreted, you may need to research the legislative history of its enactment. You can sometimes find a clue in the first section of a chapter where that statute is found, which may spell out the purpose of the law. You can also learn about the legislative history of a law by noting bill numbers and other references in the text and in the pocket parts. If you look up those enacted bills in the session laws, you can sometimes learn a little more about the legislators' reasoning and intent. The best sources of legislative history, however, are the reports published by the committees that examined and worked on the bill as it was winding its way through the legislature. Hearings and records of debate are also a good place to discover what the bill's sponsors had in mind and how they expected it to be applied.

Legislative history is important when trying to convince a court what a legislature or specific legislator meant when a law was enacted. If any ambiguity exists that has not been dealt with in the case law, you can refer to committee reports, the debates on the floor of the legislature or even testimony given by witnesses before legislative committees as evidence of the intent of the authors of the law. For most research, you will not have to concern yourself with legislative history.

Some states are much better than others about making this sort of information readily available. If you decide to look for legislative intent, first see if any court cases have already examined these documents. If you wish to delve into them yourself, it is recommended that you find a copy of a book or article that explains how to do legal research in your state to find out if reports and other legislative history materials are even published.

For federal legislative history research, see Chapter 10.

Federal Statutes

Some legal concerns are governed by federal statutes or by the government regulations that specify how those statutes should be applied. Always check to see if federal statutes or regulations apply to your problem or question. Source materials for federal laws are easily located and relatively easy to use. As with state law, checking the statutes before you explore case law will probably help you narrow your case-law research.

Keep two things in mind as you read this chapter. First, researching federal statutes is not as complicated as it may appear. You may have to look at several different sources with similar sounding names, but these materials are published in a logical pattern, and that logic will become apparent once you start using the materials. (You must have these materials in front of you to understand this chapter.)

Second, there's a good chance that you do not have to worry about researching federal statutes at all. Most legal problems, such as divorce, probate, neighborhood disputes and the like involve state law. If the techniques described under *Locating Federal Statutes* below fail to produce anything that applies to your situation, you needn't plow through the materials on federal regulations. If any federal laws or regulations apply to your situation, they will usually show up in your research of case law.

Before you begin this chapter, glance at *Statutes and Codes* and *The Arrangement of Codes* in Chapter 9 if you haven't done so already. Although written in the context of state statutes, these two sections largely apply to federal statutes as well.

OFFICIAL AND UNOFFICIAL SOURCES

Laws passed by Congress are published in both official and unofficial sources. *The United States Statutes at Large* is the official reporter of

Congressional legislation and is where you will find the session laws (called Public Laws at the federal level). The *United States Code (U.S.C.)* is the official codification of these statutes. The most recent volume of both the *Statutes at Large* and the *U.S.C.* will likely be a few years out-of-date, as these series generally run behind the actual enactment and codification of the statutes.

Unofficial sources are the *United States Code Annotated (U.S.C.A.)* and the *United States Code Service (U.S.C.S.)* published by West and LexisNexis, respectively. Besides their useful annotations, their major advantage is that they are published quickly and therefore are more up-to-date than the most recent official codification. As with official state statutes and codes, the unofficial federal codes reprint the entire text of the statutes and use the same title and section numbers. Always use the unofficial annotated codes if they are available.

ARRANGEMENT OF THE U.S. CODES

The *U.S.C.* and the two unofficial codes are all arranged in exactly the same way. The *U.S.C.* is broken into 50 titles, which are further broken down into chapters and sections, much like state codes. All three codes contain a title-specific index at the end of each title, a large general index and additional tables and finding aids. The unofficial codes add some extra tables, such as a *U.S.C.S.* table that refers you to related rules in the *Code of Federal Regulations (more on regulations is found in Chapter 11)*.

Citations to the *U.S.C.* will look like: 29 USC 651. Here, "29" is the title (labor laws), "U.S.C." is the source—the *United States Code*—and "651" is the section. If you have a citation to the *U.S.C.*, you can use it with *U.S.C.A.* or *U.S.C.S.* as well. 29 USCA 651 and 29 USCS 651 will be the exact same law—plus annotations.

U.S.C. is updated differently than the other two versions of the code. *U.S.C.A.* and *U.S.C.S.* both employ the traditional pocket part/supplement method, which is expanded upon below. On the other hand, *U.S.C.* is issued every six years and is updated in between by entire new volumes called supplements that are issued a year at a time. For instance, the code was issued in 1994. In 1995, supplement 1 was released, in 1996, supplement 2 was released, and so on, until 2000, when the code itself was reissued, incorporating all of the changes from the intervening supplements. Updates to the I trickle in a title or two at a time, and tend to run several years behind the present, making it a dangerous set to use when current information is needed. At the time of this writing, the *U.S.C.* on the shelf was three years out-of-date.

LOCATING FEDERAL STATUTES

If you think your problem may involve federal statutes, go directly to the *U.S.C.A.* or *U.S.C.S.* For example, if you have a problem at work that the *Occupational Safety and Health Act* (OSHA) might cover, you can do the following:

1. If you are following a reference from another source, you'll already know that OSHA is in Title 29, Sections 651 to 678. Go directly to the most recent edition of the *U.S.C.A.* or *U.S.C.S.* and find the appropriate volume.

2. If you're interested in a particular act (such as OSHA) and happen to know its name but not its location, look in one of the following places.

• The *U.S.C.A.* includes a complete popular name table located in a separate volume after the General Index. It also has a "Popular Name Acts" list at the beginning of each title, but this list only contains the acts included in the title covered by that volume. The U.S.C.S. has its complete popular name table in one of the Tables volumes that follow the General Index volumes.

• If you don't have access to either of the unofficial codes, the *U.S.C.* has a similar table entitled *"Acts Cited by Popular Name."* Some years it is included in Title 50, while in others it may be in a separate volume. Look for *"Popular Names Tables"* written on the spine of the book and use the most recent one you can find.

• Shepard's *Acts and Cases by Popular Name* includes both federal and state materials and is edited to include only the names of those acts and cases that the editors consider most important. It is organized alphabetically and is updated regularly.

3. If you had a job-related safety question but did not know that OSHA existed, you could search for the appropriate material in one of two ways:

(A) Look in any volume of the *U.S.C.A.* or *U.S.C.S.* for the Titles of the United States Code index, which is typically on the first or second page of every volume of each of these collections, or scan the spines of the titles on the shelves. In the list of titles, you will see "29. Labor." The Title 29 volumes in the *U.S.C.A.* and *U.S.C.S.* all contain a table of contents and indexes that lead you to OSHA.

In the *U.S.C.A.*, Title 29 fills a number of volumes. Page one of each volume has a complete list of chapter topics for that title. Chapter 15 (Occupational Safety and Health) begins with section 651. The spine of each volume shows which sections it contains. (You want the one that contains section 651.)

The *U.S.C.S.* covers Title 29 in many volumes as well. It has a table of contents at the beginning of each volume that tells you the section number for each chapter. Each chapter begins with a detailed section-by-section description.

Browsing your way to a statute in this manner is a good way to get started, but if you come up empty-handed, be sure to still look in the index to be sure you haven't missed something *(see below)*. Even if you do find a statute on your topic, you should still look to make sure there aren't any others.

(B) If you don't know the name or citation for an act, use the General Index of the *U.S.C.A.* or *U.S.C.S.*, just as you would use the general index of a state code to find the title, chapter and section that has the information you need. A key word such as "safety" would eventually lead you to the appropriate material.

If you have found relevant material using one of the techniques described above, it often helps to double-check your research by looking in the General Index to see if you have missed any leads.

READING TEXT

Once you find the appropriate title and section, read the statute. The full texts of statutes are reprinted in the *U.S.C.A.* and the *U.S.C.S.* For laws too recent to be codified, there are supplements at the end of *U.S.C.A.* and *U.S.C.S.* which print them. Also, the pamphlets at the end of the *United States Code Congressional and Administrative News (U.S.C.C.A.N.)* are a good source for newer laws. The *U.S.C.* is official and should be cited in preparing any document for a court or other official tribunal, but it is often a few years out-of-date. The annotated codes are unofficial, but they cross-reference other materials that can be helpful, and they are current. Generally, these cross-references are to materials by the same publisher, so it is best to discuss the two annotated codes separately.

UNITED STATES CODE ANNOTATED

West's *U.S.C.A.* reprints each title of the *U.S.C.* section-by-section with extensive historical notes, annotations, referrals to secondary materials, cited cases and references to West topic and key numbers. The *U.S.C.A.* is updated and reissued in hardcover title-by-title. Some libraries mix old and new versions of the same title on the same shelf, so be sure to get the most recent volume available. Update all information in that volume using either the pocket part or the most recent cumulative *Supplementary Pamphlet* at the end of the title.

To update, check at the back of the volume for a current pocket part. Then, look at the end of the general index for the *Interim Pamphlets.* These are separate paperbacks with a red spine that report all changes up to the end of the preceding year.

UNITED STATES CODE SERVICE

LexisNexis's *U.S.C.S.,* like West's *U.S.C.A.,* reprints each title section-by-section. Each section is followed by references to secondary sources, form books, law journal articles and court decisions that have interpreted the section. Also available are references to the *U.S.C.* and the *Code of Federal Regulations (CFR)* discussed in the next chapter.

For updates, the *U.S.C.S.* uses pocket parts and paperback supplements. A monthly paperback *Advance Book* (found at the end of the collection) updates new laws, administrative regulations, executive orders and the like. As with *U.S.C.C.A.N.'s* updates *(see below),* these paperbacks are not cumulative, so you must check each month's edition. The *U.S.C.S. Advance Book* also has a *"Table of Code Sections Amended, Repealed or Otherwise Affected"* that updates title sections by referring you to the new law's number. To find that new statute, look in the other issues of the *U.S.C.C.A.N.* or the *Advance Book.*

Besides its General Index, the *U.S.C.S.* contains the rules of procedure for regulatory agencies, such as the Securities and Exchange Commission, the Occupational Safety and Health Administration (which administers OSHA), the Social Security Administration and the like. These rules are found in the Code of Federal Regulations (CFR), but the *U.S.C.S.* version contains helpful cross-references and research guides to encyclopedias, *U.S.C.* citations and other resources that make the rules easier to understand. Again, don't forget to check the pocket parts. Also check the most recent *U.S.C.S. Advance Book's* "Table of Administrative Rules of Procedure Changes." This cumulative table notes all changes for each regulatory agency, so you need only to look under an agency's name to see if any supplementary volume's information has recently changed.

For the novice, the *U.S.C.S.* makes it easier to locate the additive rules and regulations that implement the title and section you are researching.

Be prepared, however, to use *either U.S.C.A.* or *U.S.C.S.,* because not all law libraries have both. The important thing to remember is that merely updating legislation may not end your search. After passage, legislation has to be implemented. In the course of this implementation, the executive branch may develop another body of law—executive and administrative rules and regulations. These will be discussed in the next chapter.

AN EXAMPLE: USING AN INDEX TO FIND STATUTES

Remember from Chapter 9 that the steps to locating a statute in a code are:
- begin with the index;
- find the code section(s) in the main volumes of the code;
- check for annotations and other helpful information; and
- update the section(s).

The following is an example of how to use the index in the *U.S.C.A.* The steps, however, apply to any code that you use, regardless of whether it's a federal or state code. If you choose to follow the example but don't have access to the *U.S.C.A.*, use *U.S.C.S.* if you can; otherwise, the *U.S.C.* will do.

This example is based on the materials available as of August 2003. You'll probably find more recent supplements, pocket parts, index volumes and so on when you do your research, but the techniques will stay the same.

For this example, imagine that you work in a small office and feel that you have been denied a promotion on the basis of your race. You're concerned that the civil rights laws may not apply to your employer because of the small size of your workplace.

Start with your initial word list. In this case, you might think of "civil rights," "discrimination," "employer," and "race." Any of these might get you going.

You look up "civil rights" in the index (located at the end of the set). This is a pretty large topic, so there are a lot of subheadings.

You find the subheading for "Equal employment opportunity," and if you skim down the page, you will see an entry that reads "Employer, definitions, 42 § 2000-e." This means that at Title 42 of *U.S.C.A.*, section 2000e, you will find the definition of "employer" under the equal opportunity laws.

Now find the volume of title 42 that has that section in it. (In August 2003, that volume was 42 *U.S.C.A.* §§2000e to 2000e-4.) Turn to the page where §2000e starts. Note that this is the definitions section of the statute, and if you look at (b), you will discover that the term "employer," as used in the statute, means a workplace that has 15 or more employees. A few pages after this, you'll see the historical information, followed by the "Library References"—references to secondary materials such as law review and encyclopedia articles. Finally, there are the notes of decisions for this section of the statute. These are the descriptions of the cases that interpret this section, and you might want to see if any cases further flesh out what qualities an employer must possess in order to be subject to this law.

Before you put the volume away, make sure you check the pocket part in the back to see if the law has been amended or repealed. The pocket part will also refer you to more recent cases and other materials. You use it by looking up section 2000e, just as you did in the main volume. If there's nothing in the pocket part for your section (which is not the case in this instance), then your law hasn't been updated before the pocket part was published. You also should consult the pamphlets at the end of the code to see if there's anything even more recent.

UNITED STATES CODE CONGRESSIONAL AND ADMINISTRATIVE NEWS

To learn about any legislation too recent to be included in the updates to either annotated code, you must use West's *U.S. Code Congressional and Administrative News (U.S.C.C.A.N.). U.S.C.C.A.N.* can also help you find the text and legislative history of recent congressional acts that may interest you.

Basically, *U.S.C.C.A.N.* contains all statutes in U.S. Statutes at Large plus a partial legislative history for most acts (usually consisting of committee reports and studies or excerpts from these). *U.S.C.C.A.N.* is published year-ly, the first one or two volumes containing the statutes enacted in the most recent session of Congress, the remainder containing the legislative history of those statutes.

The tables and indexes in the last volume of the *U.S.C.C.A.N.* can be espe-cially helpful. One of these—"U.S. Code and U.S. Code Annotated Sections Amended, Repealed, New, Etc."—allows you to learn whether the title and sections you are concerned with have been affected by new legislation. For each section affected, a page number is given. This is the actual page number in one of the first two volumes of the collection where you can find the statute that caused the change.

If you have used all of the current supplements for the *U.S.C.A.* or U.S.C.S., you need only check the most recent *U.S.C.C.A.N.* Supplementary Pamphlets (found at the end of the set) to update your information. In fact, you may not have to research any further than the "*U.S.C.* and *U.S.C.A.* Sections Amended" tables in the most recent pamphlets on the shelf.

CHAPTER 11

Administrative Law

The executive branch of government actually has two major parts: the executive office of the president, governor, mayor or other elected official and the administrative departments that are under the executive's authority. These administrative departments and agencies run the day-to-day operations of the government. Both of these parts of the executive branch have law-making authority.

Executive and administrative law comes from three primary sources:

1. *Executive orders and proclamations* from the president, a state governor or other executive.

2. *Rules and regulations* from federal and state administrative agencies and departments.

3. *Rulings and opinions* from administrative agencies.

The importance of federal and state administrative regulations can't be overstated. For example, if you are applying for a state or federal agency benefit program, these are the rules that will be used to decide your eligibility. Always check first with the agency to determine whether it has plain language handbooks that describe procedures. It could save you considerable time. Also, a good introductory text to administrative law may help clarify some of the procedures if you anticipate extensive contact with an agency. *Administrative Law in a Nutshell* is one such book.

EXECUTIVE ORDERS

Presidential proclamations and executive orders (E.O.s) are virtually synonymous terms for orders that involve limited matters, such as appointments, or far-reaching policies, such as non-discriminatory hiring practices for government contractors. These orders are published in several places, such as the *Weekly Compilation of Presidential Documents* (for orders issued since 1965), *The Public Papers of the Presidents* (from the Hoover administration forward, excluding F.D. Roosevelt), the *Federal Register,* Title 3 of the *Code of Federal Regulations (CFR)*, LexisNexis' *U.S.C.S.* and West's *U.S.C.C.A.N.* Presidential orders are usually general and vague and must be implemented by executive agencies through rules and regulations. Because of this, it is usually best to focus your administrative law research on the *CFR,* discussed below, and turn to presidential documents only if you are specifically directed to them by the *CFR.*

State and local-level executive law operates in much the same way. Unfortunately, few libraries have these proclamations codified in a volume. If you need to find such an order from a state or local official, be sure to call the library first to see whether it has the information. If not, try calling the library in your state capital or in the local city or town hall and ask if a copy of the order can be mailed to you. State executive orders may be available through state home pages on the Internet as well. *(See Appendix II.)*

FEDERAL RULES AND REGULATIONS

Administrative agencies have rules to govern their operations internally and to carry out their missions, such as the regulation of an industry. Often, the rules and regulations are written by the agency itself and are reviewed by a legislative committee that oversees the operation of the agency. These rules are important if you have any dealings with an administrative agency.

Code of Federal Regulations. Federal agency rules and regulations are published annually in the *Code of Federal Regulations (CFR).* These are grouped by subject titles that correspond somewhat to the federal agencies involved, such as Transportation, Health and Agriculture.

The *CFR* has 50 titles, most of which do not correspond to *U.S.C.* title numbers. In other words, conservation laws can be found in title 16 of the *United States Code,* but environmental regulations are in title 40 of the *CFR.* Each title consists of one or more volumes subdivided into chapters, parts and sections. Parts are designated by the symbol §, sections by a decimal point. "§ 151.6" refers to section 6 of part 151. A sample citation to the *CFR* reads as follows:

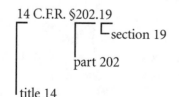

14 C.F.R. §202.19
└ section 19
part 202
title 14

Although the *CFR* titles sometimes correspond to *U.S.C.* titles, the part and section numbers do not. If you are researching OSHA in Title 29 of the *U.S.C.*, the OSHA-related regulations will be in title 29 of *CFR*, but you would have to consult the index in *29 CFR* to continue your research. If you are researching a subject in *U.S.C.* that is not covered in a corresponding volume of *CFR*, you will have to use the *CFR Index*. Even if the titles do correspond, it's possible that your topic may also be covered elsewhere in the *CFR*, so checking the Index is a good idea.

The *CFR Index* contains a table of statutory and *U.S.C.* authority for *CFR* sections. If you know, for example, the *U.S.C.* section numbers that relate to your topic, you can use this table to find the appropriate *CFR* section numbers. And if you know only the Public Law number of a federal statute, you can also use this table to find the appropriate *CFR* sections.

The Index volume also contains the subject index for the *CFR*. References are to title and part, however, not to specific sections. LexisNexis publishes a much more detailed index called the *CIS Index to the Code of Federal Regulations,* which can lead you directly to the sections that you need. Not all libraries will have this multi-volume index, but if yours does, it should be located either right before or right after the *CFR* on the shelf.

CFR is revised annually, a few titles at a time. In theory, about 12 titles of the *CFR* are updated every quarter during the year, but unfortunately, the revisions are often several months late. A list of "Sections Affected" in the back of each *CFR* volume shows which sections in that volume were modified during the previous year.

To update a *CFR* section to see if any changes have occurred since the title was last revised, look in *Cumulative List of CFR Sections Affected (LSA).* This is a paperback published each month. It includes all changes since the last annual revision of the title that you are researching. Each month's *Cumulative List* indicates all sections that have been affected in any way and gives the *Federal Register* page number where the change is reported. *(See below.)* Bold numbers indicate changes made during the prior year, while unbolded numbers are pages from the current year's *Federal Register.* Proposed changes are also noted, along with the *Federal Register* page number for the notice of the proposed change. The list of sections affected does not include the text of the changes, however. For that, you must turn to the *Federal Register.*

To update the most recent month's *Cumulative List of CFR Sections Affected* look at the "Cumulative List of Parts Affected" in the latest daily issue of the *Federal Register.* This covers any changes made or proposed during the current month. Depending on the latest *LSA* available, you may need to look in the last issue of the month for prior months as well.

Like all publications that issue from the government, however, it may take a while for a library to receive *LSAs* and *Federal Register* issues. Regulations can be updated to the present day using the Government Printing Office's Web site at *www.access.gpo.gov. (See Appendix II.)*

Federal Register. The *Federal Register* began publication in 1936 and is published daily. It includes the texts of new agency rules and regulations, proposed rules and regulations and a calendar of the meetings and proceedings of all federal rule-making bodies. The *Federal Register* also publishes the text of Executive Orders and Proclamations.

Each issue of the *Federal Register* groups documents under five headings: Presidential Documents, Rules and Regulations, Proposed Rules, Notices and Sunshine Meetings. The section on Rules summarizes each rule enacted and cites the affected title and chapter numbers of the *CFR*. Depending on the effective date and other matters, the section may also contain the complete text of the rules change. The Proposed Rules section reports proposed changes in the same manner. The Notices and Sunshine Meeting sections report mostly calendar information and announcements about public hearings.

The *Federal Register* is most useful for two types of research. The first is to find new regulations that have not yet made their way into the *CFR*. The other is to read an agency's comments about a particular rule, which can be extensive. These comments form the reasoning behind a regulation, and may explain how to apply it. Comments are not included in the I when the regulation is published there.

STATE RULES AND REGULATIONS

Most state and some local governments publish their rules and regulations in an administrative code. There may also be an administrative register for your state or locality. It may be similar to the *Federal Register* but is probably published less frequently. Locate the volumes into which the reports are compiled and select the most recently published one. In addition, many agencies place their rules online. You can find state agencies through the state home page and may be able to find a locality's agencies through the locality's home page. See Appendix II for information about how to locate a state homepage. If you do use rules that you find online, make sure they are current.

RULINGS AND OPINIONS

Statutes and administrative regulations are frequently tested and interpreted by courts at all levels. They are also the subject of hearings by specially created review boards called quasi-judicial forums. These forums, usually created by statute, hear disputes involving the application of a particular administrative agency's regulations. For example, the Occupational Safety and Health Administration reviews disputes that arise under OSHA rules and regulations, the National Labor Relations Board hears claims of violations of the National Labor Relations Act and the Federal Communications Commission handles matters that arise from interstate and international communications issues.

The proceedings of these quasi-judicial forums are like those of traditional courts, although often less formal. The federal forums were created to lighten the caseload of the federal courts and to allow the people affected to resolve disputes over federal regulations more efficiently.

Many states have also created quasi-judicial forums to help their courts cope with the growth of state regulatory law. An additional advantage of such a quasi-judicial system is that this is where the "nuts and bolts" of future legislation and subsequent regulations are often worked out in practical terms.

In the federal system, quasi-judicial proceedings may be reviewed by Administrative Law Judges, Courts of Appeals and, ultimately, the U.S. Supreme Court. States have similar patterns of appeal although it varies from state to state.

The rulings of quasi-judicial forums at the federal level are published in bound volumes, advance sheets, pamphlets and bulletins. A reference to a ruling by a quasi-judicial forum should tell you the case number and the proper volume of the hardcover report series to look in. For example, a decision of the National Labor Relations Board (the federal agency that decides labor-management disputes) might be cited as:

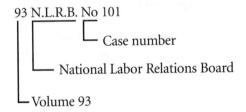

93 N.L.R.B. No 101
└ Case number
└ National Labor Relations Board
└ Volume 93

The publishing format of these decisions varies from agency to agency. Some include only the text of the decisions, some add their rules of procedure, others also include related court decisions. Boards and commissions have their own rules and procedures for how they operate. These are published in the *CFR*. Again, these rules are crucial if you have to go before one of these agencies for any reason.

Federal quasi-judicial forum decisions are also reported unofficially in loose-leaf services and, occasionally, in more comprehensive series, such as annotated codes. Loose-leaf services were discussed in Chapter 6, and a list of loose-leaf services is given in Appendix III.

The difficulty in researching state decisions in this area is that many states do not publish reports of their quasi-judicial proceedings. If you have trouble finding quasi-judicial rulings on the implementation of a particular state statute, the best approach is to contact the administering agency directly.

CHAPTER 12

Understanding Case Law

C ase law is usually the last source of information to turn to when trying to answer legal questions. That is because it's the hardest kind of research. For this reason, use secondary sources, too, as your key to case law research. *(See Chapter 6.)* Nevertheless, you will probably have to turn to case law to see if the statute or administrative law you've located is current, to see how it is usually applied to cases like yours or to learn how the courts have resolved problems that are not specifically covered by statute or regulation.

Finding case law that is related to your general problem is easy, but finding the court decisions that will help you answer specific questions (especially about the possible outcome of an anticipated court case) will take more careful research. This is largely because of the intricate structures of the court systems and the way their rulings are published, along with the vast number of cases that are decided each year.

As stated in Chapter 4, case law is the law the courts "make" by their rulings. Federal and state appellate and supreme court opinions are published in case books or *reporters*. Only a few trial court judges issue written opinions so you will be primarily concerned with appellate and supreme court opinions.

Once a court issues an opinion, that opinion becomes an authority on cases in that jurisdiction that present similar facts and similar issues. Thus, if a judge in an Alabama Court of Appeals rules one way on a point of law and a judge in Georgia rules the opposite way on the same point, your case in Alabama will be bound by the precedent set by the Alabama judge. The only way an existing precedent can be changed is by a higher court's ruling. That's why it is important to always look for the highest available court opinion.

The five most important things to keep in mind as you prepare to look for relevant case law are jurisdiction, facts, holding, mandatory and persuasive authority and citation form.

JURISDICTION

A court must have both personal and subject matter jurisdiction in order to hear a case. Personal jurisdiction means that the court actually has authority over the parties based on their citizenship or activities within the locality in question. *In rem* jurisdiction is the power of the court over the property involved in the dispute. Subject matter jurisdiction means that a court has the authority to enforce the laws that are at issue in a particular case.

From the brief discussion in Chapter 4, remember that jurisdiction therefore limits the "territory" of a court in three ways: it creates a geographical limit; it limits the subject matter of cases that can be heard; and it limits the power of the court in relation to higher courts. For example, a traffic court in Worcester, Massachusetts, can hear cases that occur only within that city, but the Massachusetts Supreme Judicial Court can hear cases that arise anywhere in Massachusetts and the U.S. Supreme Court can hear any case that involves federal issues from anywhere in the United States.

Under the second limiting concept (subject matter) the Worcester Traffic Court can only hear cases that involve violations of that city's traffic code; it cannot decide landlord tenant disputes, contract cases, employment issues or anything else. The U.S. Supreme Court's subject matter jurisdiction, on the other hand, can extend from the constitutionality of the Worcester traffic code to the extent of presidential power, but it can only review cases that in some way concern constitutional or federal questions or other clearly-defined subject areas.

The third limit involves original and appellate jurisdiction. The structure of the nation's court systems provides for decision-making on several levels, with each level subject to review by a higher court. A court which hears a case first is said to have *original jurisdiction*. Those courts that hear cases on appeal from lower courts are said to have *appellate jurisdiction*.

The important thing to remember is that most courts' decisions can be appealed at least once. To win an appeal, the dissatisfied party in the original trial must convince an appellate judge that an error was made by the lower court.

Suppose, for example, that the traffic court in Worcester has always accepted the written testimony of police officers as evidence in traffic violation cases. Suppose further that you are a driver who defends a case on the grounds of being improperly stopped for speeding. You protest the ticket but lose in traffic court on the basis of the written testimony of the arresting officer. At the trial, you dispute the written testimony and ask to confront the officer in court. Your request is denied.

You could appeal on the grounds that the lower court should have allowed you the right to confront the arresting officer in person. If you win on appeal, it's likely that the procedures for accepting written testimony will change in all Worcester traffic courts. However, if the city of Worcester in turn appeals the appellate-level decision to the state's supreme court, that court's decision could affect all traffic courts in Massachusetts.

A decision made by an appellate court applies to all lower courts within its geographical and subject matter jurisdiction. This is true within each state's court system and the federal court system. The federal and state court systems overlap geographically, but they are separated by the subject matter of the cases they consider. The jurisdiction of federal courts is discussed below.

FEDERAL JURISDICTION

The subject matter jurisdiction of federal courts is limited to: cases that involve the interpretation or application of federal statutes, international treaties or the Constitution of the United States; cases in which the federal government is a party; and cases between residents of different states (called *diversity jurisdiction*).

The geographical jurisdiction of federal courts is circumscribed by the boundaries of each court's district or circuit. Each state has at least one *U.S. District Court.* The larger and more populous states are divided into multiple districts, each with its own U.S. District Court. Each state, in turn, is part of a group of states that makes up a federal circuit. Each state group is called a circuit because it is part of the "circuit" that Supreme Court Justices used to "ride" when hearing appeals from the U.S. District Courts, before the intermediate Circuit Courts of Appeals were established in 1891. The *Federal Circuit Courts of Appeals* handle appeals from the U.S. District Courts. There are 13 Federal Circuit Courts of Appeals, one for each of the 11 numbered circuits, plus one for the District of Columbia and one for a special Federal Circuit, which hears appeals from specialized federal courts.

The *U.S. Supreme Court* is the federal court of last resort. Cases heard on appeal by a Circuit Court of Appeals may be appealed once more to the U.S. Supreme Court.

In addition, the U.S. Supreme Court is the court of final appeal for all court systems if the case involves an issue that falls within the Supreme Court's jurisdiction (if, for example, it involves a constitutional question), and if the court *chooses* to review a decision of a lower state or federal court.

Geographical Limits of the U.S. Courts of Appeals

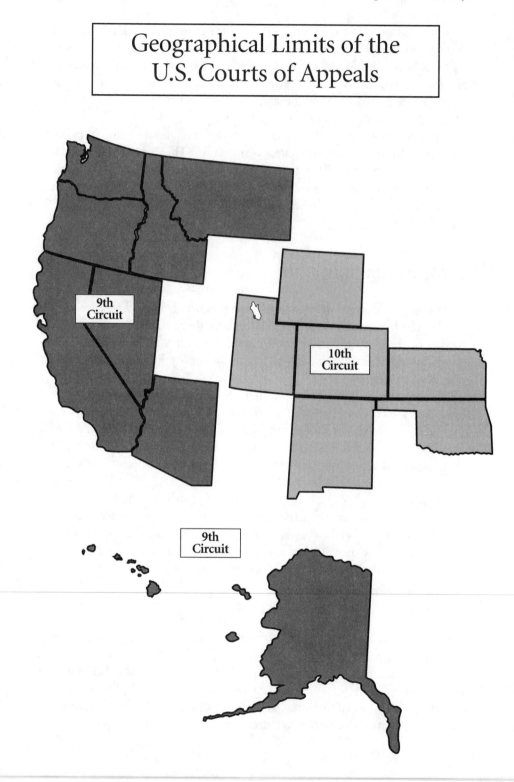

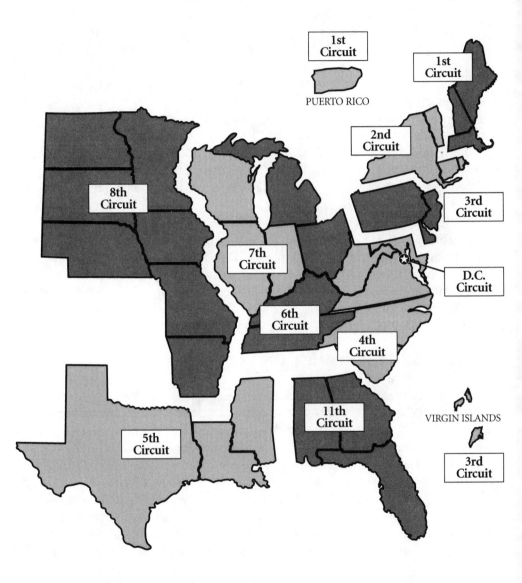

The Supreme Court may decline to hear any case for which it has appellate jurisdiction. When this happens, as it does for the vast majority of appeals, the previous court's decision stands and is the final precedent.

The U.S. Supreme Court also has original jurisdiction in a few narrowly-defined areas. Some of these are defined in the Constitution and others in statutes. They include disputes that involve two states as parties, ambassadors and public ministers, litigation between the federal government and a state and litigation between a state and the citizens of another state or a foreign country.

In September 1988, the U.S. Congress passed a law that drastically reduced the original jurisdiction of the U.S. Supreme Court (the cases the court is *required* to review). This law eliminated many categories of original jurisdiction cases and now treats those cases the way the court treats all others, through its discretionary appellate jurisdiction. *(Map of the Circuit Courts of Appeals appears on pages 78 and 79.)*

Specialized federal courts deal with issues such as cases against the government (U.S. Court of Claims) and federal tax questions (U.S. Tax Court). Each of these operate like a U.S. District Court, except that their subject matter jurisdiction is limited to a distinct area. Appeals from some of these courts are made to the special Circuit Court of Appeals for the Federal Circuit.

DIVERSITY JURISDICTION

Cases often end up in federal court when they involve citizens of different states. When this happens, federal courts are said to exercise *diversity jurisdiction*. Diversity jurisdiction makes it possible for a person to bring suit in federal court rather than a state court in either party's state, providing the amount in dispute exceeds a certain amount (defined by the Federal Rules of Civil Procedure), not including interest and court costs.

If, for example, a citizen of Massachusetts is injured in a car accident by a citizen of Rhode Island and the accident occurs in Massachusetts, it is possible for the Massachusetts citizen to sue the Rhode Island citizen in a number of courts: Massachusetts state court, Rhode Island state court or U.S. District Courts in either Massachusetts or Rhode Island (if the amount of damage or injury involved exceeds the minimum requirement). Once the suit is filed, the Rhode Island citizen can have it "removed" from either of the state courts to federal court simply by asserting that the case should be heard in federal court because of the diversity of citizenship among the parties.

When they appear in a U.S. District Court, their case will be tried under the laws of the state in which the action occurred—in this example, Massachusetts. This is true whether a U.S. District Court in Massachusetts or Rhode Island hears the case. This is why you will frequently find citations to federal court cases when you research state law.

Forum Shopping. Lawyers sometimes go "shopping" for jurisdiction, because occasionally the state and federal courts that share jurisdiction over a case have marked differences in their precedents—their history of case law. If a state and federal court share geographical and subject matter jurisdiction over your case, it is to your advantage to choose the court system that has the clearest and most favorable rulings for people in situations similar to yours. You also may consider things such as which court is more convenient to you and which court can get you to trial quicker.

Understanding how jurisdiction works is important because it will help you locate and evaluate the relevance of case law decisions. If you know which courts have geographical and subject matter jurisdiction over your case or problem, and if you understand which is the highest court and which is the lowest, then you can narrow your search for case law to a few volumes. The techniques for case law research will be discussed in the next chapter. (For a more detailed discussion of jurisdiction and court systems, see HALT's *Citizens Legal Manual,* **Courts & Judges.**)

STATE JURISDICTION

State courts also have jurisdictional limits, and courts at the trial-level hear cases brought by one citizen against another or by an out-of-state citizen against an in-state citizen. Usually these trial-level courts are divided into divisions or branches that deal with subject areas—such as domestic relations, probate or criminal law.

Above these are appellate courts and above them is a court of last resort, usually called a supreme court.

State courts have the authority to hear all cases that are not exclusively reserved to the federal system. All cases that involve state law can be heard in state courts. A typical state system is California's, illustrated in the chart below, taken from HALT's *Citizens Legal Manual,* **Courts & Judges**.

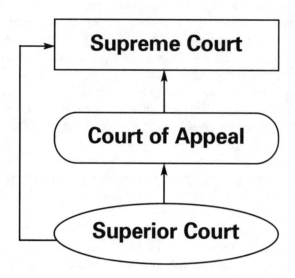

FACTS

The facts, or *fact pattern*, of a case are the particulars of the situation that brought the parties to court. These are usually set out in the first part of the decision, although additional facts may be mentioned throughout. Since the duty of the judge is to apply the law to a set of facts, cases that deal with the same area of law but have dissimilar fact patterns may be *distinguished* from each other and, therefore, decided quite differently. On the other hand, if the facts of two or more cases can be united through *analogy*—that is, if the court can say that apples are like oranges because they're both fruits—then these seemingly different cases may result in the same outcome.

When preparing for a trial where a unique set of facts will be presented to the court, researchers try to find cases to which they can make analogies and distinctions. With these cases, they will argue to the court how the law should be applied and why.

HOLDING

The *holding* of a case is the narrow statement of a court's final decision about the exact question that the court was asked to answer. When an appeals court reviews a case, it passes judgment on the actions of the lower court. The appeals court's holding *affirms* (approves), *concurs* (agrees with the lower court's decision, but for different reasons), *reverses* (decides that the original loser should have won) or *remands* (returns the case to the lower court). If a case is remanded, another full or partial trial or review may be ordered to be conducted according to the ruling issued by the appellate court. A case may also be remanded to the lower court with instructions to issue an order that implements the decision of the appellate court.

The holding sometimes begins with "We hold..." or "In this case we find...." Sometimes it simply says, "Reversed" or "Affirmed," which means that you must know the decision of the lower court to understand what was decided. The holding is ultimately what counts; the remainder of the opinion is called *dicta*. Dicta may explain the reasoning behind a decision, but the holding is what is important—it is the "bottom line."

When searching case law for an answer to your question, you must find cases in which the courts examined situations like yours. When you find cases in which the series of events or facts that caused the dispute are either identical or exactly analogous to those in your situation, the cases are said to be *on-point*. That is, they are virtually identical to your case, not merely relevant.

On-point cases are important to yours because of the court's commitment to following precedent. It makes them reluctant to decide identical situations in a way that differs from prior courts' decisions. An on-point holding from a court in your jurisdiction that reviewed an identical case is the key element you are looking for in answering your legal questions. However, be aware that the "magic bullet" case may be elusive and, in the end, may not exist.

MANDATORY AND PERSUASIVE AUTHORITY

The appellate structure of our court system is based on two principles: first, higher courts are able to override the decisions of lower courts and, second, an appellate court decision applies equally to all lower courts within its jurisdiction. This is to ensure that the law is evenly and consistently applied throughout a given jurisdiction.

To return to our Worcester Traffic Court example, if the Supreme Judicial Court of Massachusetts agrees with the intermediate-level appeals court that written testimony is inadequate in traffic court proceedings, then the rule for *all* Massachusetts traffic courts is that written testimony may not be substituted for a personal appearance by an arresting officer.

In making the decision, the Massachusetts Supreme Judicial Court is exercising its authority over lower courts within its jurisdiction. It has mandated that the Worcester Traffic Court, and all other traffic courts in Massachusetts, accept its ruling. The ruling is *mandatory authority*: it must be followed.

Mandatory authority is created: (1) when the legal issues in question have been decided by the same court or by a higher court within the same jurisdiction; (2) when the issues are constitutional and the U.S. Supreme Court has decided them (here the Supreme Court's subject matter jurisdiction covers all courts in the U.S.); or (3) where the issues are governed by state or federal statutes, administrative rules or regulations or rules of procedure.

Persuasive authority is the collection of judicial opinions, decisions and so on that may be used to influence a court's decision but that the court is not obliged to follow. In case law, the reasoning and holdings of court decisions can be used only as persuasive authority in courts of separate jurisdiction. For example, a case identical to yours may have been tried and settled in the Tennessee Supreme Court, but if your case is in Massachusetts, any decision reached in Tennessee is—at best—persuasive authority.

The decisions of "co-equal" appellate courts of separate jurisdictions are also merely persuasive, not mandatory, authority. In the federal court system, for example, the decisions reached in the U.S. Court of Appeals for the First Circuit are not mandatory authority for the Second Circuit or any of the other circuits. The flow of mandatory and persuasive authority is easier to understand if you examine the chart for the federal court system below.

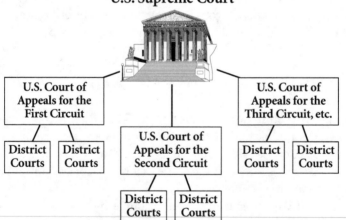

U.S. Supreme Court

A decision of the U.S. Court of Appeals for the First Circuit is mandatory authority only for the District Courts that are within the First Circuit. A decision of the U.S. Supreme Court is mandatory for all of the Circuit Courts and all of the District Courts below them, but decisions of the First Circuit Court have no direct bearing on the Second Circuit Court or its lower courts. A holding of the First Circuit Court may persuade a judge in the Second

Circuit Court to reach a similar decision, but it cannot force the judge to do so. If judges in the First and Second Circuit Courts of Appeals reach opposite conclusions on similar matters (called "a split in the circuits"), then the U.S. Supreme Court may decide to review one of the cases. The U.S. Supreme Court's decisions would then be mandatory authority for all circuit and district courts below and uniformity would thereby be established.

The *reasoning* behind a ruling of an appellate court's decision is only persuasive authority even within that court's own jurisdiction. Only the holding of a higher court is mandatory on lower courts.

An appeal is usually made on a particular point of law. A judge's ruling on that particular issue is mandatory on lower courts, but the judge's reasoning or comments on other aspects of the case are also only persuasive.

Finally, the arguments or analyses of dissenting or concurring judicial opinions, or of legal scholars in law journals, legal encyclopedias, treatises and so on may also be used as persuasive authority. Of course, a court does not have to follow such persuasive authority when making a decision, but in the absence of on-point case law or statutory law, judges are often willing to follow the reasoning of other judges or experts in a particular area of law. (Remember to cite secondary authority to a court very sparingly, though, and avoid referencing legal encyclopedias and the like.)

CITATION FORM

A *citation* (or *cite*) is a case name and a group of numbers and letters that tells you where to find that case. The case is named after the parties involved—as in *Smith v. Jones*. In the original trial, the *plaintiff's* name (the party who is suing) appears first, while the *defendant* (the party being sued) is second. The letter "v." is an abbreviation for *versus*, which is Latin for "against."

The order of appearance of the names may change at the appeal stage. The loser in the first trial is usually the initiator on appeal, and so the loser's name appears first. ("Loser" is somewhat misleading because the "winning" party can also appeal, if the winner is dissatisfied with, for example, the size of the final award.) Just remember that the first name given in an appeal case citation may be the original plaintiff or defendant, depending who was dissatisfied with the verdict of the lower court.

To confuse things further, appeals courts sometimes use different terms to identify the parties. Whichever side appeals (plaintiff or defendant) is now called the *petitioner* or *appellant* while the party defending itself becomes the *respondent* or *appellee*. Use of these terms depends on the rules and customs of the court involved.

Matching the names of those involved with their roles at the appellate stage is sometimes difficult, but it is essential to do if you are to understand the meaning of a case's holding. Because most of the cases you will be examining will be appellate-level cases, think of *Smith v. Jones* as *petitioner versus respondent* (or *appellant versus appellee*). The text of the case report will explain who was whom in the original case.

If Smith was the plaintiff in the original trial and the appellate case of *Smith v. Jones* was affirmed, then Smith "lost" twice. That is, the lower court's decision against Smith has been upheld. Conversely, if *Smith v. Jones* was reversed at the appellate level, then Jones has "lost." If Jones then appeals to the state's supreme court, the case may be called *Jones v. Smith.*

The names of the parties in a citation is called the *caption.* It is followed by a series of numbers and letters that indicate the publications in which the case has been reported. Often a case will be included in several case-law collections (or *reporters*). When this occurs, the caption is followed by more than one citation. These are called "parallel citations," as in this example below:

Sun'N Sand. v. United Cal. Bank, 21 Cal. 3d 671, 582 P. 2d 920,148 Cal. Rptr. 2d 329 (1978).

The first number in a publication cite is always the volume number. This is followed by the standard abbreviation for the reporter cited. The page number is last. The year the case was decided is in parentheses at the end of the citation and the various publication citations are separated by commas. Thus, the above citation may be broken down as follows:

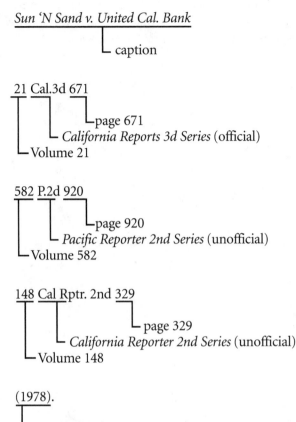

Sun 'N Sand v. United Cal. Bank
 └ caption

21 Cal.3d 671
 └page 671
 └ *California Reports 3d Series* (official)
└Volume 21

582 P.2d 920
 └page 920
 └ *Pacific Reporter 2nd Series* (unofficial)
└Volume 582

148 Cal Rptr. 2nd 329
 └ page 329
 └ *California Reporter 2nd Series* (unofficial)
└Volume 148

(1978).
└Date decided.

Reference books that give citations usually explain them in abbreviations at the front or back of the book. A complete list of standard abbreviations for reporters, codes, law journals and the like can be found in *A Uniform System of Citation* (popularly referred to as the *Blue Book*) or *Bieber's Dictionary of Legal Abbreviations*. Either may typically be found in the reference section of the library.

The caption of a citation is not always written in the form of *plaintiff v. defendant* or *appellant v. appellee*, however. In *re Smith*, for example is the caption for a judicial proceeding that does not involve adversary parties. Bankruptcy, probate, guardianship, contempt of court and disbarment hearings are typical *in re* cases. (*In re* is Latin for "in the matter of.")

In criminal cases, the state or federal government is considered the party wronged by the act of the defendant; the state initiates legal action against the accused. A typical caption, for example, is *State v. Smith*. Some states use

"Commonwealth" or "People" instead of "State." If the federal government initiates a case, the caption is *United States v. Smith*, but if Smith sues the federal government, the caption is *Smith v. United States*.

CHAPTER 13

Reading Case Law

You are now ready to begin researching case law. If you have followed the steps in this manual, you will probably have several case citations in hand by this point. This chapter tells you how to locate the cases for which you have citations and how to read the cases when you find them. The next chapter tells how to find additional citations in the case digests.

REPORTERS

Case decisions are published in *reporters*. A reporter is a set of books that contains case opinions from a given geographical area. Regional reporters typically are published in tan covers with black and gold lettering on tan and red spines. A single regional reporter can include hundreds of volumes.

The first few pages of each volume list the courts whose cases are published in that reporter as well as the names of the cases reported in that volume. If you are concerned with a statute, there is also a list of "Statutes Construed" in the beginning of each volume. This is a list of the statutes that have been interpreted or referred to in case decisions. The list includes both state and federal statutes. If you're researching a particular statute, these tables can give you citations for all cases published in that volume that deal with the statute.

The cases appear in chronological order according to the date each decision was announced. Every state has a reporter for its highest court. These are usually published in official versions by the state and in unofficial versions by commercial publishers. Depending on the state and the publisher, some reporters also include appellate decisions from intermediate-level state courts.

Of the huge number of judicial opinions announced each year, only a small percent of them are published. In theory, the ones selected for publication are those that make a contribution to the development of the law, not those that simply repeat its application to similar or identical cases. For this reason, the decisions of state and federal trial-level courts are rarely published. Most of the cases you read will be from appellate-level courts. Even so, more than 40,000 cases are published annually.

An opinion may be chosen for publication because it applies a legal principle to a new situation, because it reverses long-established principles of how to apply the law or because of the way it views or applies the proper application of a statute in a new way to a particular set of facts. These criteria are intended to separate the extraordinary from the routine decisions. The fact that 40,000 decisions are published each year shows how the law is constantly changing in a multitude of jurisdictions. Your task in researching case law is to discover the most recent statement of law regarding your situation in your jurisdiction.

STATE AND REGIONAL REPORTERS

Suppose your notes contain this citation: *King v. Superior Court*, 108 Ariz. 492, 502 P.2d 529, 60 A.L.R. 3rd 172, (1972). By the citation alone, you know you can read the decision on that case in three different reporters. The first (108 Ariz. 492) is the official one—*Arizona Reports*—in which the case decision appears in volume 108 on page 492. (The various citation abbreviations are explained later in this chapter.)

The second citation, 502 P.2d 529, is to an unofficial source, the *Pacific Reporter, Second Series,* which is part of the *National Reporter System,* published by West. The system includes regional reporters of state court decisions and federal reporters of federal court decisions.

Every state belongs to one of seven regions established by West *(the map and chart on pages 92 and 93 show the West system of regional reporters).* Appellate court decisions of the states within each region are printed together in that region's reporter. For example, the states of Ohio, Indiana, Illinois, Massachusetts and New York are grouped in the *Northeastern Reporter.* Because of the useful head notes and other annotations provided by the West editors, always choose the West state or regional reporter over the state's official reporter when reading a case.

The "Second Series" in these reporters are completely separate sets of volumes. For example, the *Northeastern Reporter* includes cases published in that region from July 1885 to April 1936. The *Northeastern Reporter, Second Series* contains cases from April 1936 to the present.

Both the *California Reporter* and the *New York Supplements* are special series containing cases from those states only. Besides covering the state's supreme court decisions, they also report important cases from lower appellate courts whose decisions would not ordinarily be included in a regional reporter. For example, the New York Supplements contain decisions from all New York state appellate courts since 1888, while the *Northeastern Reporter* includes only decisions of the New York Court of Appeals, the state's highest court. The *California Reporter* contains cases from all California appellate courts. It began publication in 1959; lower appellate cases decided before 1959 are found in the *Pacific Reporter*.

Another feature of the *National Reporter System* is that West's editors often choose cases that are not published in a state's official reporter. It is therefore not unusual to come across a case that has only an unofficial citation.

FEDERAL REPORTERS

Your research may lead you to federal court cases even though your situation involves only state law. Because litigants from different states can choose whether to go to federal or state courts, federal courts often find themselves interpreting and applying state law. Because each state has one or more federal court districts at the trial level and is part of a federal judicial circuit at the appeal level, you should be familiar with federal reporters.

Most federal reporters are unofficial records published by private companies. For many years, West has been the only publisher of the opinions of U.S. District Courts and U.S. Circuit Courts of Appeals. The following are the principal federal case law reporters.

U.S. Supreme Court: *United States* (official). Abbreviation: *U.S. United States Supreme Court Reports, Lawyer's Edition* (LexisNexis). Abbreviation: L.Ed. *Supreme Court Reporter* (West). Citation: S.Ct.

U.S. Supreme Court—Current Year's Session: *Commerce Clearing House Supreme Court Bulletin* (Commerce Clearing House). *United States Law Week* (Bureau of National Affairs). Abbreviation: USLW.

Circuit Court of Appeals: *Federal Reporter* (West). Abbreviation: F., F.2d. or F.3d. *Federal Cases* pre-1880 (West). Abbreviation: F. Cas.

District Courts: *Federal Supplement* (West). Abbreviation: F. Supp., or F. Supp. 2d. *Federal Reporter* pre-1933 (West). Abbreviation: F.

Suppose, for example, that you have this citation: *Primrose v. Western Union Tel. Co.,* 154 U.S. 1, 14 S.Ct. 1098, 38 L.Ed. 883, (1893). This U.S. Supreme Court decision will be reported in all of the three Supreme Court case reporters: *United States Reports* (U.S.); *Supreme Court Reporter* (S.Ct.); and the *United States Supreme Court Reports, Lawyer's Edition* (L.Ed.).

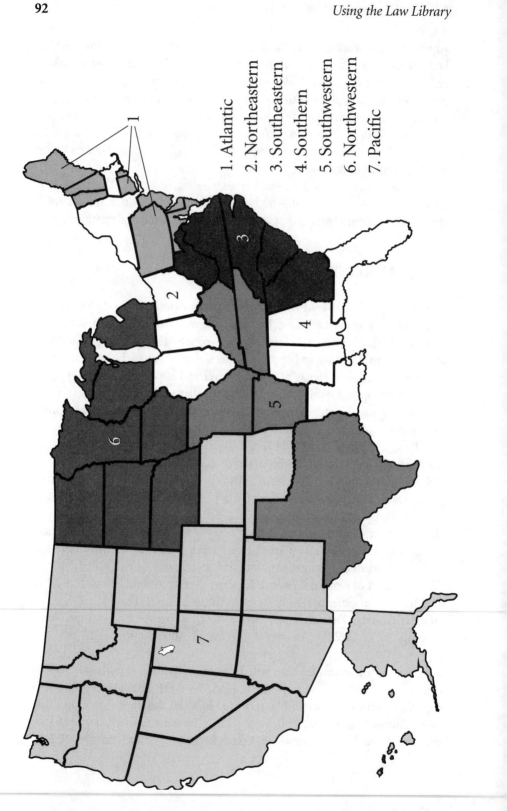

1. Atlantic
2. Northeastern
3. Southeastern
4. Southern
5. Southwestern
6. Northwestern
7. Pacific

The abbreviations for the regional reporters are as follows:

MAP #	ABBREVIATION	NAME
1	A. and A.2d	Atlantic Reporter and Atlantic Reporter, Second Series
2	N.E. and N.E.2d	Northeastern Reporter and Northeastern Reporter, Second Series
3	S.E. and S.E.2d	Southeastern Reporter and Southeastern Reporter, Second Series
4	S. and S.2d	Southern Reporter and Southern Reporter, Second Series
5	S.W. and S.W.2d	Southwestern Reporter and Southwestern Reporter, Second Series
6	N.W. and N.W.2d	Northwestern Reporter and Northwestern Reporter, Second Series
7	P. and P.2d	Pacific Reporter and Pacific Reporter, Second Series
	Cal.Rptr.	California Reporter

University law libraries are likely to have all three. Smaller libraries might have only one.

Courts of Appeals and other courts of special appeals often publish their own opinions in "slip" form (on separate sheets of paper). These are not bound or collected in a hardcover edition, so the unofficial sources (*e.g.*, West publications) are the only bound sources for federal court decisions below the Supreme Court.

All federal reporters are supplemented by advance sheets and paper-back editions published at regular intervals before being collected in hard-cover editions.

Once you find a case, be sure to shepardize it to see if it was appealed (*see Chapter 15*). Until you have traced a case to the highest court, you cannot be sure whether or not a lower court's decision is the current, "good" law. (You will also need to shepardize it to see how later courts have dealt with your case.)

The U.S. Supreme Court's current session is covered by the loose-leaf services of Commerce Clearing House (CCH) and the Bureau of National Affairs (BNA). Loose-leaf services are extremely useful sources of information about recent case decisions. Their use is discussed in Chapter 6.

Many courts and legal information Web sites place judicial decisions online. Most of these maintain a collection of cases from the mid to late 1990's on. See Appendix II for suggested resources.

AMERICAN LAW REPORTS

Besides providing a wealth of information on selected legal topics (*see Chapter 6*), remember that the *A.L.R.* also includes cases. It is **far** more selective in its choice of cases than is the more inclusive *National Reporter System*, however. The cases are chosen for their special usefulness to legal researchers. For example, a case might be chosen for publication to give editors an opportunity to analyze a major shift in an area of law, such as products liability or negligence. Or the case might be selected as a definitive statement on a very specific legal point, such as one involving fishing rights on inland lakes.

An annotation in *A.L.R.* can also help a legal researcher by analyzing related areas of law, citing to other cases and cross-referencing to digests and encyclopedias. Because the annotations take time to prepare, the most recent cases are probably not going to be found in *A.L.R.* If your preliminary research leads you to an *A.L.R.* citation, definitely read the annotation. It might save you hours of research time. Chapter 6 discusses annotations in more detail.

HOW TO READ A CASE

When a case is appealed to a higher court, both parties submit written *briefs* that summarize the facts and arguments about how the law should be applied. The attorneys for both sides can also make oral arguments in court.

Appellate courts typically have at least three judges. Some have as many as nine. After reviewing the transcript of the original trial and the arguments of both sides, a majority of the judges agrees on a decision. One of the judges is assigned to write an opinion stating the reasons for the majority's decision. Although the decision of the court is, technically speaking, only the final action of the court (affirmed, reversed, remanded, etc.) and not the written opinion, *opinion* and *decision* have become interchangeable terms.

THE STRUCTURE OF CASE DECISIONS

Although case decisions are published in a variety of state, regional and federal reporters, the one thing they have in common is the following format:

1. *The name of the case.* The names of the parties involved in the case are printed in dark bold letters at the beginning of the decision.

2. *Docket numbers.* The numbers assigned each case by each court that hears it identify the case as it moves through the system. A case usually has three such numbers by the time it reaches a state supreme court. A case heard in the Supreme Court of Oregon, for example, might have these:

No. 71-3146; CA 16098; SC 27080—the docket numbers from the trial court, from the Oregon Court of Appeals and from the Supreme Court of Oregon. Warning: *This number will not help you locate a case in a case book or reporter but may be useful for finding other information, such as briefs, orders, etc., if you determine you need them.*

3. *Date of decision.* The date of the court's decision is listed along with the date when the briefs and oral arguments were submitted.

4. *Case history.* The nature of the case is briefly summarized along with the name of the lower courts involved and the previous court's decision.

5. *Headnotes.* The legal rules or, occasionally, the significant facts of the case are summarized in *headnotes.* These are numbered, assigned to a topic and (in West publications) given a key number designation. A brief descrip-

519 U.S. 3   **CALIFORNIA v. ROY**   **337**
                              Cite as 117 S.Ct. 337 (1996)

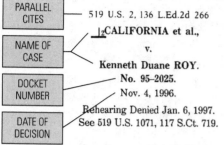

519 U.S. 2, 136 L.Ed.2d 266

⌊2CALIFORNIA et al.,

v.

Kenneth Duane ROY.

No. 95–2025.

Nov. 4, 1996.

Rehearing Denied Jan. 6, 1997.

See 519 U.S. 1071, 117 S.Ct. 719.

Petitioner sought habeas corpus relief from his California convictions of robbery and first-degree murder for aiding and abetting felony murder. The United States District Court for the Eastern District of California, David F. Levi, J., denied relief, and petitioner appealed. The Ninth Circuit Court of Appeals affirmed, 55 F.3d 1483, and rehearing en banc was granted. The Circuit Court of Appeals, James R. Browning, Circuit Judge, 81 F.3d 863, reversed and remanded, holding that erroneous omission of aiding and abetting instruction of requirement that jury find that defendant intend to encourage or facilitate principal's offense was not harmless. The state of California filed petition for writ of certiorari. The Supreme Court held that error in jury instruction that defined crime without including statement that jury was required to find that defendant had intent to commit or facilitate crime had to be reviewed by habeas court under the *Kotteakos* harmless error standard, which is whether the error had substantial and injurious effect or influence in determining the jury's verdict.

Petition for writ of certiorari granted, and Ninth Circuit's opinion at 81 F.3d 863 vacated and remanded with directions.

Justice Scalia concurred with separate opinion, in which Justice Ginsburg joined in part.

1. Habeas Corpus ⚷450.1

Federal court, reviewing state court determination in habeas corpus proceeding, ordinarily should apply the *Kotteakos* "harmless error" standard of whether the error had substantial and injurious effect or influence in determining the jury's verdict.

2. Habeas Corpus ⚷450.1

The *Kotteakos* harmless error which is whether the error had substantial and injurious effect or influence in determining the jury's verdict, does not apply to structural defects in the Constitution of the trial mechanism, but does apply review of so-called trial errors, including rors in respect to which the C requires state courts to apply a stricter, *Chapman*-type standard of "harmless error" when they review a conviction directly.

3. Habeas Corpus ⚷450.1

If judge, in habeas proceeding, applying *Kotteakos* harmless error standard, which is whether the error had substantial and injurious effect or influence in determining the jury's verdict, is in grave doubt as to the harmlessness of an error, habeas petitioner must win.

4. Habeas Corpus ⚷498

Error in jury instruction that defined crime without including statement that jury was required to find that defendant had intent to commit or facilitate crime was an error of omission or so-called trial error, as opposed to structural error that defies analysis by harmless error standards, and thus, error had to be reviewed by habeas court under the *Kotteakos* harmless error standard, which is whether the error had substantial and injurious effect or influence in determining the jury's verdict.

⌊3PER CURIAM.

A California court convicted respondent Kenneth Roy of the robbery and first-degree murder of Archie Mannix. The St[ate's the]ry, insofar as is relevant here, was coming to the aid of a confederate trying to rob Mannix, helped the confederate kill Mannix. The trial judge gave the jury an instruction that permitted it to convict Roy of first-degree murder as long as it concluded that (among other things) Roy, "with knowledge of" the confederate's "unlawful purpose" (robbery), had helped the confederate, *i.e.*, had "aid[ed]," "promote[d]," "encourage[d]," or "instigate[d]" by "act or advice ... the commission of" the confeder-

tion of the legal rule involved is also included, along with a citation to the statute, if the rule is based on a statute.

Headnotes do not appear in all cases. Cases published by West and LexisNexis will include them, but many government-published reporters will not.

A typical West headnote, from an Oregon Supreme Court case, appears as:

2. Parent and Child (◯⟿) **3.1(1)**
Child support may take forms other than
direct monetary contribution. ORS 107.105(1)(b).

In the word index of a case digest *(discussed in Chapter 13),* under the heading *Parent and Child,* you will find cites to dozens of cases that address the general issue. If you look instead in a West digest under the number (◯⟿) 3.1(1), you would find cites only to cases which have dealt specifically with child support issues.

The "2" before the topic category is an important time-saver. Some court decisions may address a multitude of legal issues and have a headnote for each. In this case, "2" is the headnote number and corresponds with the number at the beginning of those paragraphs of the judge's written opinion that discuss the legal issue summarized in the headnote. This makes it easier for you to focus your attention on that point of an opinion that you are interested in.

The headnote number is also useful in a second way. Each legal issue considered in a case may also be considered in subsequent court cases. This means that to update completely all of the issues in a case, you might have to read 20 to 30 later cases. However, because what you really want to do is update only the legal points you are interested in, you can use this headnote number as a shortcut when you update by *shepardizing (discussed in Chapter 15).* The important thing to remember at this stage is to keep track of these headnote numbers as you take notes on the legal issues you're researching in case law. It is also useful to note that West puts the collection of cases in key number order in the back of each volume of its reporters.

Headnotes are intended to serve merely as an index to the points of law discussed in an opinion. Usually written by the editors of the reporter, they are a useful guide to the opinion, but they are not the law. The editors can make mistakes, so always read the judge's opinion to be sure that the headnotes accurately reflect the decision. And, because the facts of a case always affect its result, simply stating a rule of law cannot fully explain why a specific decision was reached in a specific case. Not only must you read the case to check the accuracy of the headnotes, you must read the entire case to see precisely how the legal rules were applied.

6. *Names of counsel and judges.* The names of the lawyers for both parties in the suit are followed by the names of the judges who heard the case. The name of the judge who wrote the opinion is given before the opinion begins.

7. *Opinion of the court.* The opinion usually begins with a statement in which the judge describes what the case is about and what legal issues the court was asked to decide. The remainder of the opinion discusses the legal issues individually.

The opinion represents the view of the majority of the appellate judges who heard the case. A member of the majority may agree with the decision but disagree with the reasoning behind it, however. That judge may write a concurring opinion printed after the majority opinion. The minority may also write a dissenting opinion explaining why it disagrees with the majority opinion. A dissenting opinion may be written by an appointed member of the minority, or each dissenting judge may write a separate dissenting opinion. Dissenting opinions are not binding as precedent. They are considered dicta and have merely persuasive authority. See Chapter 12 for more details.

8. *The decision or holding.* This is the "bottom line" that indicates how the court ruled on the case. The case may, for example, be "affirmed," "reversed" or "remanded."

Not all of the above elements will appear in every case report. For instance, you may not find a case history or headnotes in an official reporter. Access to headnotes is one of the best reasons for preferring unofficial over official reporters.

ANALYZING CASE DECISIONS

The most important task in reading a case is to extract the information you need without getting bogged down in extraneous material.

This is not always easy. The written decision of the court may be veiled in unfamiliar jargon and elaborate discussions of other cases may be buried within the decision. Judges discuss other cases to show that their decision is consistent with previous decisions in similar cases. However distracting it may be to read carefully accounts of the *fact patterns* and decisions of many other cases, it can also help you understand how the law developed in a particular area. If the cases cited look particularly promising—because of the closeness of their facts to those in your situation or because of the importance of their impact on the law—make a note of them for further reading.

Another difficulty may be that it isn't apparent why you are reading a particular case at all. The facts may be quite different from those in your case, for instance, but you have been led down this trail by your research for some reason, so don't give up too quickly. At some point you should be able to connect your case with the one you're reading. The essential information you need might appear as little more than a judge's comment that, "If the facts of the case had been such and such (exactly your situation)..., we would have decided thus and so...."

The following offers one basic approach to reading a case. You'll probably want to tailor this to fit your own research style after you've had some practice.

1. *Don't spare the paper.* Start taking notes on each new case with a fresh sheet of paper that gives the case name and all citation information.

2. *Be sure to copy the cites* for both the official and unofficial reporters. Write down parallel citations at this point. It will save you from having to use only one reporter if you need to return to the case later.

3. *Read carefully through the fact summary* at the beginning of the opinion. This is your first clue to how similar the facts of this case are to those of your situation.

4. *Write down the issues* as they are presented by the judge. Unfortunately, the facts are not always presented in the most direct way. In most cases, the judge usually says something such as, "The issue in the case is..." or "The questions presented are..." or "Plaintiff/Defendant contends that...." The way the issues are defined by the court will determine how they are settled. If your notes record the specific questions posed and answered by the court, you may be able to understand what may appear to be contradictory findings in other cases. Headnotes can help you identify issues by listing all of the important points of law at the beginning of the case. For instance, you may find a case that has a headnote that reads "Ex-wife's remarriage terminated former husband's obligation to pay alimony, despite a non-modification agreement between both parties."

5. *Take complete notes.* Judges often explain at length the principles upon which their decisions are based. For you, this is the meat of the case, because in giving the historical basis, the judge places the facts of this particular case within the context of "the law." This is what you're after. Often, judges cite additional cases for each legal proposition. You'll eventually learn to choose only

the propositions that directly relate to your situation but, in the beginning, write down the important points so you won't have to retrace your steps.

Suppose your car's brakes, recently repaired, fail and result in damage to your car. You want to sue both the mechanic who fixed your brakes and the service station. As you research similar cases, you might spend considerable time reading about the law of agency and "respondeat superior," even though you got to these cases by following the trail of "negligence law." However tempted you might be to exclude the material on agency from your under-standing of your situation, in this case it would be a mistake. Whenever you run into an unfamiliar concept, stop and do a little basic research on it, or, at the least, take good notes on all references to it and pursue them later.

6. *Write down the citations.* As you find general legal propositions you believe are important to your case, write down the citations related to the propositions. Experience will teach you what to ignore, but taking notes is always easier than making return trips to the library or to volumes you have already searched.

7. *Make sure you understand who won and why.* This is not always clear, because judges frequently use labels instead of names, and the role of each party (appellant, appellee, plaintiff, defendant, plaintiff-in-error, respon-dent-in-error and so on) changes in some courts as the case passes through the levels of appeal.

It also often happens that a judge will spend considerable space leading up to a decision on a case similar to yours and then decide the questions on a procedural point that doesn't apply to you. If you are simply educating your-self about the law, this kind of decision won't trouble you. If, on the other hand, you are trying to build a legal argument, a decision against your posi-tion (even with the most supportive commentary) can be a liability to your argument.

8. *Look for cases with facts that are on point with yours.* You are also look-ing for case support from the highest courts within your jurisdiction, includ-ing the U.S. Supreme Court. These issues are discussed in detail in the previ-ous chapter, and it is essential that you understand them before you immerse yourself in case law.

9. *Make sure the cases you research are good law.* This is the most impor-tant reminder and bears repeating. Are the cases you are reading still current law? To determine this, you must use *citators* such as *Shepard's* or *Keycite* to update them. *Shepardizing* is discussed in Chapter 15.

CHAPTER 14

Case Digests

Our discussion of case law to this point assumed that your research through statutory materials and secondary sources produced citations to relevant cases. Each of these cases may lead you to others, since most opinions are replete with references to other cases. It may be, however, that none of the cases cited by judges or legal authors is relevant to your inquiry. If the cases you've referred to don't answer your questions, you'll have to look for other cases in the *digests*. A digest is a directory of case law that is organized by subject matter. Another way to think of it is as an extremely large, detailed index to case law.

WEST'S KEY NUMBER SYSTEM

To use the digests discussed in this chapter, you need to understand West's *key number* system. West has divided all law into seven main groups called classes. These are subdivided into subclasses, which are further divided into topics. Altogether, there are hundreds of topics, each of them further divided into very specific numbered subtopics, called key numbers (aptly named because they "unlock" the West digest system). Each topic may have from a handful to hundreds of key numbers associated with it.

West editors read cases, identify the points of law touched on in each case and decide where each of these points fits into the enormous variety and number of legal topic categories that make up the digest system. The editors then assign the appropriate key numbers to those points of law, along with a sentence or two about that point of law as applied to the case. Together, the topic, key number and the short description that follows make up a headnote. When you look up a topic and key number in a digest, you'll find the headnotes for cases that have been assigned that topic and key number. The digest will also give you the citation to the case so that you can look it up in the reporter.

Because the topic and key number system is truly that—a system—might be helpful to review the discussion of headnotes in the previous chapter to understand how it all fits together.

There are several benefits to using the key number system to find cases. One is that each key number is assigned to a very narrow point of law, so the cases you find when using that number will deal with that precise topic. For instance, you don't want to read every negligence case ever decided in your jurisdiction when you're only concerned with whether a business owner is required to take special care to make sure her floors and entryway are level and free of hazards.

Another huge benefit of West's system is that the topics and key numbers that you find are *portable*. For example, say you research your topic and don't find any cases from your jurisdiction that fit your particular situation. However, an encyclopedia (or other source) leads you to a case from another state that happens to be on-point. You can find the topics and key numbers from the headnotes belonging to the on-point case and look them up in a digest that covers your state to see if any similar cases have been decided. In other words, once you have a topic and key number, it will describe the same exact sort of issue regardless of which West digest you're using.

FEDERAL DIGESTS

If you know your legal question involves only federal case law, you can use a federal digest. If your question involves state law, you also may want to check a federal digest to make sure federal law is not involved or that federal courts haven't interpreted the state law you're concerned with under a diversity jurisdiction case. If your research topic is not covered in the indexes of the *USC, CFR* or the federal digests, you can be certain that you are dealing only with a state law question.

West has three digests that cover all the federal courts. The *Federal Digest* covers all federal case decisions up through 1938, the *Modern Federal Practice Digest* includes cases from 1939 to 1961, the *Federal Practice Digest 2d* continues from 1961 to 1975, the *Federal Practice Digest 3d* covers 1975 to the early 1980s, and *Federal Practice Digest 4th* picks up where the 3d series left off and continues to the present. The digests contain cases from the U.S. Supreme Court, the U.S. Circuit Courts of Appeals, U.S. District Courts and some specialized courts, such as the Bankruptcy and Claims Courts. The decisions of these forums are usually reported only by loose-leaf services. *(See Chapter 6.)*

The federal digests have their own descriptive word indexes, case-name tables and an index to the words and phrases defined in the cases. Even if you already know some of the key numbers that apply to your topic, check the federal descriptive word indexes just to make sure that you haven't missed topics that may be unique to federal law.

As you have probably gathered, you may need to use several digests to find all the federal case law on a given topic. But in most cases, you will want the most recent law, so begin your research with the *Federal Practice Digest 4th*. If that resource does not yield case law, you can try the earlier sets.

Each series' "Descriptive Word Index" only covers cases digested within that series. Check the indexes from each set as you use it, because topics and key numbers have changed over time as the law has developed in newer fields, such as civil rights and consumer protection. There are tables in the digest that allow you to convert from old topic and key numbers to new ones.

Supplementary pamphlets to the *Federal Practice Digest 4th* are issued every two months. Be sure to use these, found at the end of the digest, along with the pocket parts in the back of the volumes.

An example. Say you're investigating whether you are entitled to Social Security disability benefits from the federal government. You had applied for it and were turned down on the premise that you had never been hospitalized since the onset of your condition and, therefore, your situation did not rise to the level of a disability as recognized by the federal government.

You first look up your terms in the *Federal Practice Digest 4th* "Descriptive Word Index," which leads you to Social Security (⊙⟿) 140.10. Turning to the beginning of the Social Security topic, you will find a couple of outlines of the topic. The first of these outlines is general, while the second one breaks out all of the subtopics and indicates the key that corresponds with each. Using these outlines, you can quickly find related key numbers to look up.

After the outline, the headnotes are arranged in numerical order by key number. When you turn to Social Security (⊙⟿) 140.10, you will find a number of cases' headnotes reprinted along with their citations. These are arranged by court, from highest (U.S. Supreme Court, if any cases came from there) to lowest. Pay attention to jurisdiction, as well as the level of the court that decided the case. As explained throughout this book, these are critical factors to consider when trying to figure out how much weight a court will give it.

The headnotes often contain enough information for you to determine whether you need to read the case.

Sometimes you will look up a key number to find that it is followed not by a headnote, but by "See Topic Analysis for scope" or "For cases see the *Decennial Digests*." This means that no cases have been assigned that topic and key number in the digest for the jurisdiction that you're using. Go back to the sub-analysis outline. The key number you were following will be surrounded by related key-numbered topics. Try following any other key numbers that might possibly lead you to the cases you need. If you still cannot find citations that look useful, return to the "Descriptive Word Index" and try using other words from your word list to track down the answers you need. In a pinch, you can try to find persuasive authority from other jurisdictions using another digest with the same topic and key number, but it's much better to try to stay within your own jurisdiction.

SUPREME COURT DIGESTS

If you are only interested in locating U.S. Supreme Court decisions, there are two special digests which can help you. West publishes the *U.S. Supreme Court Digest*. This digest includes all of the Supreme Court cases listed in the *American Digest System*. It uses the key number classification system, contains a "Descriptive Word Index" and is updated by cumulative annual supplements.

The *U.S. Supreme Court Reports Digest* is published by LexisNexis. This digest does not use the key number system, but it does have a word index, table of cases, etc.

STATE DIGESTS

There are case digests for every state except Nevada, Delaware and Utah. Nevada publishes its own official case-law digest. For a digest of cases in Delaware or Utah, you need to use the appropriate regional digest or the *American Digest System*. The case digests for North Dakota and South Dakota are combined in *West's Dakota Digest*. The Virginia and West Virginia Digests are also combined. State digests are generally located near the state's case-law reporter in the law library.

State digests usually include all reported state court decisions and all federal cases that involve or apply state law. If your state digest does not include relevant federal cases, remember to check the federal digests before concluding your research.

Most state digests fill several volumes and include a "Descriptive Word Index" or "Topic Index," a table of the names of the cases digested and a "Words and Phrases" section that will lead you to those cases that define legal terms important to your case. Like so much else in legal research, the digests are updated by replacement volumes, cumulative supplements and pocket parts.

Each state digest begins or ends with a "Descriptive Word Index," which usually fills several volumes by itself. Using the most useful words from your word list, just as you did while checking the General Index to the state statutes, will lead you directly to the appropriate sections of the digest.

State digests are arranged in much the same way as the federal ones. Each section in the digest starts with a lengthy outline of the types of cases digested, followed by the headnotes for that topic numerically arranged by key number.

If you can't find any applicable cases or statutes, it's appropriate to look at case law from other states to see if their courts have considered similar questions of law. The ruling of other state courts would be persuasive, not mandatory authority, but they would at least indicate how a judge might decide in your situation. Because common law usually has developed along regional lines, the case law of nearby states tends to be more useful than that of distant states. To learn about court decisions in nearby states, you'll need to use those states' digests, the regional digest or the *American Digest System*.

REGIONAL DIGESTS

West publishes case digests that correspond to the regions in its *National Reporter System*. Like state digests, the regional digests follow the key number classification system.

Each regional digest covers the case reports in every state within its assigned region. The case descriptions under each key number are arranged alphabetically by state. The regional digests (like the regional reporters) cover only state case law.

The regional digests are the *Atlantic Digest (First and Second Series), South Eastern Digest (First and Second Series)* and *North Western Digest (First and Second Series)*. Other regional digests have since been discontinued and are of use only for locating decisions reported through their final years of publication.

THE AMERICAN DIGEST SYSTEM

Besides the state and regional digests, West also publishes the *American Digest System*, which includes case law from the federal courts and all 50 states—anything published in the *National Reporter System*. They are organized by date, so pay attention to the coverage year(s) as noted on the spine of each volume. As with other digests, the cases are not printed in their entirety. Instead, headnotes are used.

The *General Digest* of the *American Digest System* lists the case headnotes alphabetically by general topic. Following this, the key numbers that correspond to the subtopics within that topic are listed in numerical order. The *General Digest* is produced monthly and is bound at regular intervals. The *General Digest* is itself compiled into what are called *Decennials,* originally at 10-year (and currently at 5-year) intervals.

Once you have identified the key numbers you need, finding citations to other cases becomes easier. You can find citations to cases by looking in the *Decennials* and in the most recent yearly and monthly supplements. In each *Decennial,* first locate the topic (such as "Wills") and then the headnotes under the appropriate key number. This will give you an exhaustive list of cases.

Reading all the cases related to your problem could take forever, so you must be selective. As with any other digest, once you've carefully read the headnotes, try to select those that will be most instructive and important. In general, the more recent, the better. Also remember that decisions of the highest court within your jurisdiction carry the most weight.

Because the *General Digest* is such a huge (and, to some, daunting) set of volumes and the fact that there are certainly better alternatives to try first— such as a digest for your state—this set is best employed as a last resort. Besides the enormous number of cases digested, another problem with the *General Digest* is that a large number of volumes must be consulted while searching, since each volume only covers a specific time period. This doesn't mean that it shouldn't be used, but you should exhaust all other sources before you invest several hours in searching through the *General Digests.* For example, legal encyclopedias (especially the *A.L.R.*) can be especially useful for finding cases that would yield persuasive authority from other jurisdictions.

CHAPTER 15

Updating Cases and Statutes

Throughout this manual we have repeatedly mentioned the term *shepardizing*, a term and activity coined especially for legal researchers to mean the updating of a case or statute to make sure it's still good law. In particular, this term refers to using *Shepard's Citators*, which are available in print, on CD-ROM, and on *LexisNexis.com.* (*Westlaw.com* offers an online-only citator called *Keycite.*) Whenever you use case law (or statutory law, for that matter), that law should be updated. This chapter explains how to do that.

Updating has one goal and two uses. The goal is to make sure the case or statute you are reading has not been overturned or modified by later case decisions. The two uses are to see how the law has developed through later cases and to find cites to other sources that analyze or explain the same points of law.

You can save time reading case decisions by turning to a citator *before* following a case citation to a reporter. If the case cited has been overturned by a later case, you can go directly to the later case. This gets you to the most recent holding on your legal question. You may still need to review the earlier case because decisions are overturned on any number of grounds, and the parts of the case that deal with the line of reasoning regarding your topic may still be in good standing.

Shepardizing is named after John Shepard, the original creator of the citators. Shepard's, which is now owned by LexisNexis, produces citator volumes for state, regional and federal case reporters, and for state and federal statutes and constitutions, as well as a few miscellaneous volumes.

In your library, Shepard's may be found either all in one place or at the end of each set of reporters or federal statutes. These are large books, even by law library standards. The main volumes are maroon, with cumulative annual or semi-annual supplements that are yellow or gold paperback, and more frequent supplements that are either red or on newsprint. You may also find blue "express updates" with the citator.

The most important part of shepardizing is to check all the editions, especially the most recent. This can be tricky, since your case may be listed in the main volume, the bound supplement(s), the gold pamphlet, the red supplement and the newsprint supplement. To ensure that the Shepard's that you're using contains everything it is supposed to, take the most recent update you can find—usually either a red or a newsprint paperback edition—and check the box on the front cover. This will list all the volumes you should look at to bring you up-to-date. (Sometimes, just after a new yellow or gold *Annual Cumulative Supplement* has been issued, there will be no red or paperback supplements. The yellow *Annual Cumulative Supplement* will be up-to-date on its own.) The box is titled "What Your Library Should Contain." The volumes it lists will be dated by the years they cover. Collect and check them all. Also, make sure that the latest update is from within a month or two of the current date. If not, ask a library staff member to make sure there are no new updates waiting to be processed and added to the shelf.

Be aware that most lawyers and law students now update cases online using the two big legal databases, Lexis (which publishes the online version of Shepard's) and Westlaw (which offers *Keycite*, a competing product). Unfortunately, these are not available for free, although you can pay to shepardize or check *Keycite* with individual cases. The result of this shift from print Shepard's, though, is that some libraries, especially in times of budgetary hardship, are no longer carrying the full range of Shepard's citators since the bulk of their patrons can use the online versions. If you find that you need a citator that is not available, ask a librarian if there is a Lexis or Westlaw password for public patrons to use to shepardize or check *Keycite*.

STATE AND REGIONAL CITATORS

Shepard's publishes a case and statute citator for almost every state. It also publishes a case citator for each of West's regional reporters. The regional citators give cites to all cases reported in the National Reporter System. This can be useful in checking how other states' courts have used or interpreted the case decision you are shepardizing.

The state citators are easier to use if you are shepardizing primarily to see if your case or statute has been overturned or amended because they will only include cites to cases from your state (and related federal) courts in addition to cites to law reviews. In contrast, the regional citators (for the regional reporters) will also give you cases that are found in any regional reporter, which may be a much longer list and will include more persuasive (as opposed to binding) authority. The state case and statute citators are published in separate volumes and, depending on the state, may have both hard-cover and paperback supplements.

FEDERAL CITATORS

Shepard's has three principal federal citator sets. *Shepard's United States Citations: Statutes* shepardizes each article and section of the U.S. Constitution, the *USC, U.S. Statutes at Large,* U.S. treaties and federal court rules. You can use it to search for later amendments, interpretive case law and even articles in encyclopedias and law journals.

Shepard's Federal Citations shepardizes lower federal court cases that are reported in the *Federal Series* (and its later series) and *Federal Supplement* (and its later series).

Shepard's United States Citations: United States Reports shepardizes U.S. Supreme Court decisions from the *United States Reports* series. *United States Citations: Supreme Court Reports* and *United States Citations: Supreme Court Reporter Lawyers' Edition* are two additional citators you can use to shepardize U.S. Supreme Court cases, depending on the citation you have, since the volume and page numbers for all three of these reporters do not correspond.

READING A CITATOR

The introduction to each hardcover volume of Shepard's citations includes helpful sample citations and explanations of the format and abbreviations used. It is well worth your time to look through these pages.

The Shepard's volumes consist of pages of numbers that you will recognize as citations. The top of each page of the citator gives the name of the reporter, constitution, state code and so on that is being updated. The volume number of the reporter (or section number of the statute) being updated is printed in large type at the upper-left or -right corner of each page.

The page numbers for each reporter volume and subsections for each case, statute or article are listed in large bold numbers (such as **-828-**) followed by a list of several citations. These citations include: (1) the official and unofficial citations of the case you are shepardizing, including citations to the same case or appeals, if any; (2) citations to any treatment or reference to the case by state or federal courts in other cases; and (3) citations to law journals and materials such as the *A.L.R.*

The citations to the treatment of the case by other courts sometimes begin with letters that indicate what effect, if any, the later action had on your case.

Each citator volume includes an explanation of these abbreviations at the front. Those of major interest to you are **c** for "criticized," **d** for "distin-guished," **e** for "explained," **f** for "followed" and **o** for "overruled." This last category is critical. By reading cases that overruled the one you're research-ing, you can find the newest interpretation of the law and why the previous ruling was rejected. The references to the legal journals and other materials may also help explain the change in the law.

You can also use Shepard's to get citations to other case reporters. Shepard's translates official citations into unofficial citations and vice versa. Those in parentheses at the beginning of each entry are the parallel cites. These are given for all reported cases in bound volumes of the citators, but not in the paperback supplements.

Even individual case headnotes from West reporters can be shepardized. Headnotes were discussed in Chapter 13. If you're interested in shepardizing the point of law summarized by headnote number 7 in a case decision, for example, look for the number 7 in superscript after the citations in the list of cases cited in Shepards. Look at the following list:

554	SE2^7	678
j556	SE2^9	263
j556	SE2^2	264
j556	SE2^8	273
588	SE2^6	274
588	SE2^2	280
588	SE2^7	302

In this example, the point of law in headnote 7 was discussed in the case reported in volume 554 of the *Southeastern Reporter 2d* on page 678. The point of law from headnote 9 from your original case was discussed in a dis-senting opinion (indicated by the "j" before the volume number) in volume 556 of the *Southeastern Reporter 2d* on page 263.

At first glance, citators look impossible to read and are as dense as tele-phone directories, but they are one of the legal researcher's most useful resources and they are essential to accurate research. If you read the "illus-trative case" and "illustrative statute" examples in the preface to a Shepard's citator, you will have no trouble learning how to shepardize.

LexisNexis also publishes a pamphlet that shows you step-by-step how to shepardize. If you don't see a copy of it near the citators, ask a librarian if the library has one you can use. The pamphlet, which covers print, CD-ROM and online shepardizing, is also available online at *www.lexisnexis.com/infopro/ reference/Shepards/shep.pdf.*

A page from the Southeastern Reporter

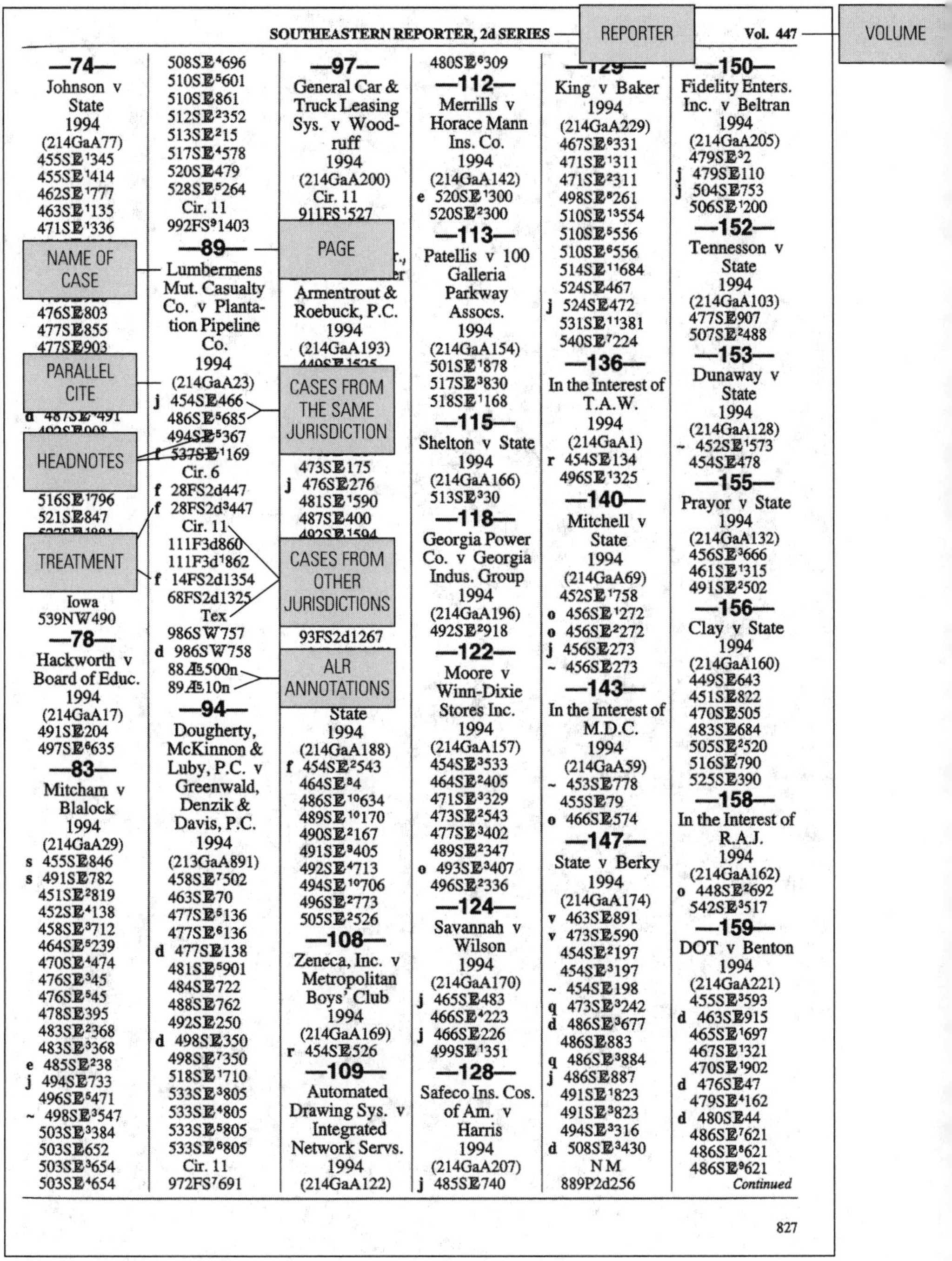
REPORTER
VOLUME
NAME OF CASE
PAGE
PARALLEL CITE
CASES FROM THE SAME JURISDICTION
HEADNOTES
CASES FROM OTHER JURISDICTIONS
TREATMENT
ALR ANNOTATIONS

SOUTHEASTERN REPORTER, 2d SERIES — Vol. 447

—74—
Johnson v State
1994
(214GaA77)
455SE[1]345
455SE[1]414
462SE[1]777
463SE[1]135
471SE[1]336
476SE803
477SE855
477SE903
516SE[1]796
521SE847
Iowa
539NW490

—78—
Hackworth v Board of Educ.
1994
(214GaA17)
491SE204
497SE[6]635

—83—
Mitcham v Blalock
1994
(214GaA29)
s 455SE846
s 491SE782
451SE[2]819
452SE[4]138
458SE[3]712
464SE[5]239
470SE[4]474
476SE[3]45
476SE[5]45
478SE395
483SE[2]368
483SE[3]368
e 485SE[2]38
j 494SE733
496SE[5]471
~ 498SE[3]547
503SE[3]384
503SE652
503SE[3]654
503SE[4]654
508SE[4]696
510SE[5]601
510SE861
512SE[2]352
513SE[2]15
517SE[4]578
520SE479
528SE[5]264
Cir. 11
992FS[9]1403

—89—
Lumbermens Mut. Casualty Co. v Plantation Pipeline Co.
1994
(214GaA23)
j 454SE466
486SE[5]685
494SE[5]367
f 537SE[1]169
Cir. 6
f 28FS2d447
f 28FS2d[3]447
Cir. 11
111F3d860
111F3d[1]862
f 14FS2d1354
68FS2d1325
Tex
986SW757
d 986SW758
88ALR500n
89ALR10n

—94—
Dougherty, McKinnon & Luby, P.C. v Greenwald, Denzik & Davis, P.C.
1994
(213GaA891)
458SE[7]502
463SE70
477SE[5]136
477SE[6]136
d 477SE138
481SE[5]901
484SE722
488SE762
492SE250
d 498SE350
498SE[7]350
518SE[1]710
533SE[3]805
533SE[4]805
533SE[5]805
533SE[6]805
Cir. 11
972FS[7]691

—97—
General Car & Truck Leasing Sys. v Woodruff
1994
(214GaA200)
Cir. 11
911FS[1]527

Armentrout & Roebuck, P.C.
1994
(214GaA193)

473SE175
j 476SE276
481SE[1]590
487SE400

93FS2d1267

State
1994
(214GaA188)
f 454SE[2]543
464SE[8]4
486SE[10]634
489SE[10]170
490SE[2]167
491SE[9]405
492SE[4]713
494SE[10]706
496SE[2]773
505SE[2]526

—108—
Zeneca, Inc. v Metropolitan Boys' Club
1994
(214GaA169)
r 454SE526

—109—
Automated Drawing Sys. v Integrated Network Servs.
1994
(214GaA122)
480SE[6]309

—112—
Merrills v Horace Mann Ins. Co.
1994
(214GaA142)
e 520SE[1]300
520SE[2]300

—113—
Patellis v 100 Galleria Parkway Assocs.
1994
(214GaA154)
501SE[1]878
517SE[3]830
518SE[1]168

—115—
Shelton v State
1994
(214GaA166)
513SE[3]30

—118—
Georgia Power Co. v Georgia Indus. Group
1994
(214GaA196)
492SE[2]918

—122—
Moore v Winn-Dixie Stores Inc.
1994
(214GaA157)
454SE[3]533
464SE[2]405
471SE[3]329
473SE[2]543
477SE[3]402
489SE[2]347
o 493SE[3]407
496SE[2]336

—124—
Savannah v Wilson
1994
(214GaA170)
j 465SE483
466SE[4]223
j 466SE226
499SE[1]351

—128—
Safeco Ins. Cos. of Am. v Harris
1994
(214GaA207)
j 485SE740

—129—
King v Baker
1994
(214GaA229)
467SE[6]331
471SE[1]311
471SE[2]311
498SE[8]261
510SE[13]554
510SE[5]556
510SE[6]556
514SE[11]684
524SE467
j 524SE472
531SE[11]381
540SE[7]224

—136—
In the Interest of T.A.W.
1994
(214GaA1)
r 454SE134
496SE[1]325

—140—
Mitchell v State
1994
(214GaA69)
452SE[1]758
o 456SE[1]272
o 456SE[2]272
j 456SE273
~ 456SE273

—143—
In the Interest of M.D.C.
1994
(214GaA59)
~ 453SE778
455SE79
o 466SE574

—147—
State v Berky
1994
(214GaA174)
v 463SE891
v 473SE590
454SE[2]197
454SE[3]197
~ 454SE198
q 473SE[3]242
d 486SE[3]677
486SE883
q 486SE[3]884
j 486SE887
491SE[1]823
491SE[3]823
494SE[3]316
d 508SE[3]430
NM
889P2d256

—150—
Fidelity Enters. Inc. v Beltran
1994
(214GaA205)
479SE[3]2
j 479SE110
j 504SE753
506SE[1]200

—152—
Tennesson v State
1994
(214GaA103)
477SE907
507SE[2]488

—153—
Dunaway v State
1994
(214GaA128)
~ 452SE[1]573
454SE478

—155—
Prayor v State
1994
(214GaA132)
456SE[3]666
461SE[1]315
491SE[2]502

—156—
Clay v State
1994
(214GaA160)
449SE643
451SE822
470SE505
483SE684
505SE[2]520
516SE790
525SE390

—158—
In the Interest of R.A.J.
1994
(214GaA162)
o 448SE[2]692
542SE[3]517

—159—
DOT v Benton
1994
(214GaA221)
455SE[3]593
d 463SE915
465SE[1]697
467SE[1]321
470SE[1]902
d 476SE47
479SE[4]162
d 480SE44
486SE[7]621
486SE[8]621
486SE[9]621
Continued

827

Conclusion

The fact that this manual on using a law library has to devote its first chapters on how to get into a law library and that, throughout the text, it must translate legalese for the reader offers evidence that our legal system is designed to serve lawyers, not others. Terms like *et. seq.* and *Corpus Juris Secundum* are integral parts of our legal system and, for nonlawyers, make understanding how our legal system operates difficult. This book aimed to shed some light on both the research process and the results that your research leads you to.

HALT supports a variety of reforms of the legal system that would further increase people's access to legal information and enable them to understand how the system works. These include:

Free Access to Public Law Libraries. People should be able to use libraries to research legal questions. Libraries on public property should be for the use of all, not only for lawyers and law school students and faculty. Free access to public law libraries is the first place to start in empowering people to handle their legal affairs.

Plain-Language Materials. An increased number of plain-language brochures, handbooks and guides on all areas of the law will enable people to handle their legal affairs and better understand their rights.

Self-Help Materials. Self-help publishers have come a long way in making materials available to nonlawyers on many legal subjects. These do-it-yourself books need to be increased in both number and availability. With the assistance of good handbooks, many more people will be able to take better control of their legal affairs and avoid the expense of hiring a lawyer.

Over-the-Counter Legal Assistance. Court clerks should assist pro se litigants by giving out self-help instructions for many routine legal procedures—such as probate, uncontested divorces and name changes.

HALT wishes to demystify the law and the process of researching it. A manual such as this one can help people work their way through a needlessly complex system but cannot substitute for a plain-language, easy-to-use system.

Change is coming. In some areas, court clerks now distribute forms. In others, computer kiosks have been installed to provide information and forms for people using the court system. Plain-language laws are bringing the law back to the people. Government bodies open their law libraries to nonlawyers. Computerized legal research is changing how we look at the law.

These developments are all encouraging. Clearly, however, much remains to be done before consumers can call the legal system their own.

Appendixes

Bibliography

The following legal research manuals are of use to nonlawyers. Many of these should be available at a good bookstore (especially one at a college or university), public library or law library. If a given book is not on the shelf, you may be able to order it.

If you belong to a public library that does not have a book that you want to read from this list, you can probably request it through Interlibrary Loan (ILL) from another library. Your library will request the book from a lender and let you know when it has arrived for you. Contact your library to find out what its policies are regarding Interlibrary Loan.

A few of the books may have too much legalese and others may be too broad or too specific for your needs, so it's best to review any book before you decide to purchase it. We have included a wide selection of titles, hoping you will find a few that are both useful and readily available.

Remember, too, that there may be research manuals written specifically for your state. These may provide you with much more detailed information about state resources than a more general book.

AALL Directory and Handbook. American Association of Law Libraries, 53 W. Jackson Blvd., Ste. 940, Chicago, IL 60604. Annual.
A list of all members of the American Association of Law Libraries (AALL). Member libraries are listed by state, including address, telephone number, size and staff names. The list does not indicate, however, which libraries are open to the public.

Basic Legal Research: Tools and Strategies, 2nd ed., by Amy E. Sloan. Aspen Publishers, 1185 Avenue of the Americas, New York, NY 10036. 2003.
A well-illustrated book that explains many concepts through graphs, pictures from printed resources and screenshots of Web pages. Some schools use this as a textbook, though it is easily understood by non-law students.

Directory of Special Libraries and Information Centers. Gale Group, 27500 Drake Rd., Farmington Hills, MI 48331-3535. 2003.
A multi-volume list of libraries under specific subjects, such as law and business. Your public library may carry this in its reference section.

Federal Depository Libraries Directory. Library Programs Service, Superintendent of Documents, U.S. Government Printing Office, Washington, D.C. Bi-annual.
Available online at *http://www.access.gpo.gov/su%5Fdocs/fdlp/tools/ldirect.html.*
Addresses and telephone numbers for all federal depository libraries.

The Federal Register: What It Is and How To Use It.
Available online at: *http://www.archives.gov/federal_register/tutorial/about_tutorial.html.*
This online guide explains how to use the Federal Register, Code of Federal Regulations and their finding tools. It also provides a "guided tour" of each source.

Finding the Law, 11th ed., by Robert C. Berring and Elizabeth A. Edinger. West Group, P.O. Box 648, St. Paul, MN 55164-0833. 1999.
This is the revised edition of the popular book, *How to Find the Law* by Berring and Morris Cohen. It provides an excellent overview of how to use West's key number system.

Fundamentals of Legal Research, 8th ed., by Roy M. Mersky and Donald J. Dunn. Foundation Press, 395 Hudson Street, New York, NY 10014. 2002.
This is one of the "old standby" research references. It is very detailed, contains helpful illustrations and covers specialty topics such as tax and international research.

Legal Research and Citation, 5th ed., by Larry L. Teply. West Group, P.O. Box 648, St. Paul, MN 55164-0833. 1999.
Provides lots of examples and a good discussion of case research.

The Legal Research and Writing Handbook, 3rd ed., by Andrea B. Yelin, Laura L. Stapleton and Hope V. Samborn. Aspen Publishers, 1185 Avenue of the Americas, New York, NY 10036. 2002.
Written for paralegal students, this book introduces the strategies and techniques of legal research.

Legal Research: How To Find and Understand the Law, 11th ed., by Stephen Elias and Susan Levinkind. Nolo, 950 Parker St., Berkeley, CA 94710. 2003.
This is one of the best on the market. A step-by-step approach to answering your legal questions. Also contains exercises to help you apply what you're learning. Its plain-language approach makes it very accessible.

Legal Research Illustrated, 8th ed., by Roy M. Mersky and Donald J. Dunn. Foundation Press, Inc., 395 Hudson Street, New York, NY 10014. 2002.
This is the shortened version of *Fundamentals of Legal Research,* 8th ed *(see above).* Although written for law students, much of the information is useful for everyone. The many charts and graphs make the book even more understandable.

Legal Research in a Nutshell, 8th ed., by Morris L. Cohen and Kent C. Olson. Thomson/West, 610 Opperman Dr., Eagan, MN 55123. 2003.
This offers a short, easy-to-read overview of how to do-it-yourself. Used by thousands of law students, this "nutshell" paperback can be a time-saver. There is a companion Web site at *http://www.law.virginia.edu/nutshell.*

Legal Research Manual: A Game Plan for Legal Research and Analysis, 2nd ed., by Christopher G. Wren and Jill R. Wren. A-R Editions, Inc., 315 W. Gorham St., Madison, WI 53703. 1986.
A strategy for approaching just about any research problem and getting your answer. It is one of the best in the field, easy-to-read and useful for all. Though it's an older publication, much of it is still relevant.

The Legal Writing Handbook: Analysis, Research, and Writing, 3rd ed., by Laurel C. Oates, Anne Enquist, and Kelly Kunsch. Aspen Law and Business, 1185 Avenue of the Americas, New York, NY 10036. 2002.
This book contains several chapters on legal research and also includes tips on writing documents for the court.

The Process of Legal Research, 5th ed., by Christina L. Kunz, Deborah A. Schmedemann, Matthew P. Downs and Ann L. Bateson. Aspen Law and Business, 7201 McKinney Circle, Frederick, MD 21701. 2000.
A complete guide written for law students and legal assistants, though it's also useful to others.

Computer-Aided Legal Research

WORLDWIDE WEB SITES

The following is a list (by no means comprehensive) of some of the better legal research sites available for free or at a low cost to anyone with a computer and Internet access. (If you do not have a computer with Internet access, your local public library probably has one you can use). Some of these are referred to throughout this book.

The problem with composing such a list is that it is out-of-date the minute it is put together. If a link doesn't work or takes you somewhere that you're not expecting, try using a search engine such as *Google.com* or *Yahoo.com* to find the site. Another option is to find a list of links online. A good way to get a current list of legal research links is to visit any law school library's homepage.

GENERAL LEGAL SITES

Sites that contain a large amount and a wide variety of information.

Cornell University's Legal Information Institute (LII)
Web site: *www.law.cornell.edu*
LII (from Cornell Law School) provides links to or the text of the United States Code, some state statutes, administrative material, cases and concise research guides for a variety of topics.

Findlaw
Web site: *www.findlaw.com*
Owned by West, Findlaw offers a wealth of information including cases, statutes, some commentary and hundreds of links to other sites. Topical collections provide forms, articles and primary materials on specific issues of law. This is one of the best free legal sites out there.

Heiros Gamos
Web site: *www.hg.org*
Much like Findlaw, this site serves as both directory of Web sites and as a provider of links to actual laws. It is another site worth visiting.

FEDERAL INFORMATION

Cornell University's Legal Information Institute (LII)
Web site: *www.law.cornell.edu*
The United States Code, the Code of Federal Regulations, and some federal rules are available, as well as links to federal court decisions.

Findlaw
Web site: *www.findlaw.com*
Findlaw links to materials from all three branches of government as well as some non-governmental information. Some full-text is available.

Firstgov
Web site: *www.firstgov.gov*
Billed as "the U.S. government's official Web portal," this page is a gateway to all sorts of federal information, including laws, regulations and agency Web site addresses.

GPO Access
Web site: *www.access.gpo.gov*
This site, maintained by the United States Government Printing Office, contains the United States Code, the Code of Federal Regulations and its updating service, as well as presidential papers, congressional documents and other federal materials.

Guide to Law Online: United States
Web site: *www.loc.gov/law/guide/us.html*
Put together by the Library of Congress, this excellent collection of links (with descriptions) takes you to a variety of information.

Lawsource
Web site: *www.lawsource.com*
Lawsource provides numerous links to federal and state government resources.

LexisOne.com
Web site: *www.lexisone.com*
LexisOne offers U.S. Supreme Court cases from 1790 to the present and federal circuit court cases from the last five years. Extended access and the ability to shepardize cases can be purchased.

Louisiana State University Libraries' Federal Agencies Directory
Web site: *www.lib.lsu.edu/gov/fedgov.html*
This is one of the most comprehensive lists of links to federal agencies out there. You can browse by agency type or pull up an alphabetical list.

Thomas
Web site: *http://thomas.loc.gov*
Thomas (named for Thomas Jefferson) is an excellent site through which to find bills and the text of recently-passed laws.

STATE INFORMATION

Findlaw
Web site: *www.findlaw.com*

Cornell University's Legal Information Institute (LII)
Web site: *www.law.cornell.edu*

Guide to Law Online: U.S. States and Territories
Web site: *www.loc.gov/law/guide/usstates.html*
Put together by the Library of Congress, this excellent collection of links (with descriptions) takes you to a variety of information. It's organized by state.

Lawsource
Web site: *www.lawsource.com*
Lawsource provides numerous links to federal and state government resources.

LexisOne.com
Web site: *www.lexisone.com*
State cases are available for free going back five years. In addition, LexisOne provides more than 6,000 state forms for a variety of types of transactions. Extended access can be purchased.

State Homepages
Web site: *www.state.__.us* (where __ is replaced with the postal abbreviation for the state)
State governments typically publish some legal information on their Web sites. Each state's site is different, though. Follow the links for "government," "courts," "legislature," "laws," "information" and so on to find materials. Keep in mind that some information may be located on the page for the branch of government from which it originates (a code being found on the legislature's page, for instance). Any state homepage can be accessed by inserting the postal abbreviation in the blank in the above address. For instance, New York would be *www.state.ny.us*, and Missouri would be *www.state.mo.us*.

COURTS

Court Rules from Law Library Resource Xchange (LLRX)
Web site: *www.llrx.com/courtrules*
A comprehensive set of links to various state and federal courts' rules.

The Federal Judiciary's Court Links
Web site: *www.uscourts.gov/links.html*
This is a collection of links to federal court homepages.

State Court Locator
Web site: *http://vls.law.vill.edu/Locator/statecourt/index.htm*
From Villanova University's law school, this is a list of state court Web sites, including courts at the circuit and district level.

LEGAL PUBLISHERS

See Appendix VI for a listing of self-help legal publishers.

Legal Publishers List
Web site: *www.aallnet.org/committee/criv/resources/tools/list*
This is a comprehensive list of legal publishers with links to information pages or publisher Web sites.

USEFUL DATABASES

The following computer resources may be available to you in the law library and are well worth looking into.

The Catalog
To find what books the library owns, use its catalog. A link to it may appear prominently on the library's homepage or, if you're using one of the library's computers, there may be an icon for it on the computer's desktop. The library may also have dedicated catalog computers. Look for signs directing users to the catalog or ask a staff member if you can't find it.

Index to Legal Periodicals
This index covers about 625 law journals from 1981 to the present.

LegalTrac
Like the Index to Legal Periodicals, LegalTrac indexes articles from the early 1980s to the present. It covers about 900 journals and legal newspapers and includes a few full-text articles.

LexisNexis Academic
As mentioned above, this is a version of Lexis.com for non-law students and can be found in many colleges and universities. While somewhat scaled-down in comparison to its big brother, Lexis.com, LexisNexis Academic provides a significant amount of information, including federal and state cases and codes, law reviews, newspapers and so on.

LexisNexis Congressional

Most of LexisNexis Congressional is an index to legislative history, but it does offer other resources, such as the United States Code Service and congressional information. If your research requires you to look at legislative history, though, there is no better source for finding it.

WorldCat

This is a database that essentially combines the catalogs of libraries all over the United States (and some from other countries). You can use it to see what books exist on your topic, including those that your library does not own. You can also find out which library owns a particular book.

CDS, DVDS AND OTHER FIXED MEDIA

Although the general trend is to move electronic resources to the Internet, some are published on CD or a similar medium. These are only useable on one computer or on a network designed to handle them—you usually have to be in the same building as the CD, if not at a specific computer set aside for them. In other words, you'll need to go to a library to use a CD.

Many resources, especially state materials, are available on CD, so don't overlook the possibility that your library may own one or more. Check with a librarian to see what is available.

Loose-leaf Services

L oose-leaf services are an excellent source of information about the law. Law libraries usually subscribe to several. You can find a loose-leaf service for virtually every area of law. The major benefits of loose-leaf services are that they are updated regularly (monthly, in some cases) and combine case law, statutory law and regulatory law on a specific area, such as labor arbitration decisions. In addition, many include overviews and histories of subject areas.

Loose-leafs have become increasingly important as a research tool because of the explosion of regulatory law from administrative agencies. Loose-leaf services are discussed in Chapter 6.

ABBREVIATIONS FOR PUBLISHERS

Commerce Clearinghouse (CCH)
Bureau of National Affairs (BNA)
Research Institute of America (RIA)

Advertising Law Guide (CCH)
Affirmative Action Compliance Manual for Federal Contracts (BNA)
Air Pollution Control Guide (BNA)
Americans with Disabilities Act Manual (BNA)
Antitrust and Trade Regulation Report (BNA)
Bank Compliance Guide (CCH)
Bank Digest (CCH)
Banking Report (BNA)
Bankruptcy Law Reporter (BNA)
Bankruptcy Law Reports (CCH)
BioTech Watch (BNA)
British Tax Library (CCH)

Business Franchise Guide (CCH)
Business on the Internet (CCH)
Canadian Tax Reporter Library (CCH)
Chemical Regulation Reporter (BNA)
Class Action Litigation Report (BNA)
Collective Bargaining Negotiations and Contracts (BNA)
Compensation (CCH)
Computer Technology Law Report (BNA)
Construction Labor Report (BNA)
Consumer Credit Guide (CCH)
Consumer Product Safety Guide (CCH)
Copyright Law Reporter (CCH)
Corporate Accountability Report (BNA)
Corporate Practice Series (BNA)
Criminal Law Reporter (BNA)
eBusiness and Insurance: A Legal Guide to Transacting Insurance and
    Other E-Commerce Tax Report (BNA)
EEOC Compliance Manual (BNA)
Electronic Commerce and Law Report (BNA)
Employee Benefits Cases (BNA)
Employee Relations (CCH)
Employment Discrimination Report (BNA)
Employment Guide (BNA)
Employment Practices Guide (CCH)
Employment Safety and Health Guide (CCH)
Environment Reporter (BNA)
Environmental Due Diligence Guide (BNA)
Equal Employment Opportunity (CCH)
ERISA Compliance and Enforcement Library (BNA)
Estate Planning Law and Taxation (RIA)
Ethics in Government Reporter (CCH)
Fair Employment Practices Summary of Latest Developments (BNA)
Family and Medical Leave Guide (CCH)
Family Law Reporter (BNA)
Federal Audit Guides (CCH)
Federal Banking Law Reporter (CCH)
Federal Contracts Report (BNA)
Federal Election Campaign Financing Guide (CCH)
Federal Environment and Safety Regulatory Monitoring Report (BNA)
Federal Ethics Report (CCH)
Federal Tax Articles (CCH)

Financial Privacy Law Guide (CCH)
Food, Drug and Cosmetic Law Reporter (CCH)
Government Employee Relations Report (BNA)
Health Care Fraud Report (BNA)
Health Care Law Monthly (MB)
Health Care Policy Report (BNA)
Health Care Program Compliance Guide (BNA)
Health Law Reporter (BNA)
Health Plan and Provider Report (BNA)
Home Health Medicare and Medicaid Payment Reporter (CCH)
Homeland Security Briefing (BNA)
Human Resources Report (BNA)
Individual Employment Rights (BNA)
Individual Retirement Plans Guide (CCH)
Inheritance, Estate and Gift Tax Reporter - State (CCH)
Insurance Antitrust and Unfair Trade Practices Law (CCH)
Insurance Law Reports (CCH)
Intellectual Property Library (BNA)
Job Safety and Health (BNA)
Labor Law Reports (CCH)
Labor Relations Reporter (BNA)
Lawyers' Manual on Professional Conduct (BNA)
Liquor Control Law Reports (CCH)
Media Law Reporter (BNA)
Medical Research Law and Policy Report (BNA)
Medical Devices Reporter (CCH)
Medicare and Medicaid Guide (CCH)
Medicare Report (BNA)
Money and Politics Report (BNA)
Mortgage Compliance Guide (CCH)
New York Stock Exchange Guide (CCH)
Occupational Safety and Health Reporter (BNA)
Patent, Trademark and Copyright Journal (BNA)
Payroll Administration Guide (BNA)
Payroll Guide (RIA)
Payroll Management Guide (CCH)
Pension and Benefits Reporter (BNA)
Pension Plan Guide (CCH)
Personal Loan Compliance Guide (CCH)
Pharmaceutical Law and Industry Report (BNA)
Privacy and Security Law Report (BNA)

Privacy Law Watch (BNA)
Product Distribution Guide (CCH)
Product Safety and Liability Reporter (BNA)
Products Liability Reporter (CCH)
Right-To-Know Planning Guide (BNA)
Sales Representative Law Guide (CCH)
Secured Transactions Guide (CCH)
Standard Federal Tax Reporter (CCH)
State and Federal Wage Hour Compliance Guide (RIA)
State and Local Taxes (RIA)
State Banking Law Reporter (CCH)
State Environment and Safety Regulatory Monitoring Report (BNA)
State Health Care Regulatory Developments (BNA)
State Tax Guide (CCH)
State Unfair Trade Practice Law (CCH)
Tax Court Reports (CCH)
Tax Management Library (BNA)
Telemarketing Law Guide (CCH)
Toxics Law Reporter (BNA)
Transportation Watch (BNA)
Unemployment Insurance Reporter (CCH)
Union Labor Report Newsletter (BNA)
U.S. Law Week (BNA)
U.S. Patents Quarterly (BNA)
U.S. Tax Reporter: Estate and Gift (RIA)
U.S. Tax Reporter: Income (RIA)
Wage Hour and Leave Report (BNA)
Wages-Hours Reporter (CCH)
Waste Management Guide (BNA)
Water Pollution Control Guide (BNA)
Workmen's Compensation: Business Management Guide (CCH)

Law Libraries

Not all of the 358 libraries listed here are open to the public. We suggest you read Chapter 2 and follow its instructions before appearing at the front door of a law library. An asterisk (*) denotes Federal Depository Libraries as of 2003—for a complete listing of federal depository libraries, see *www.du.edu/bdld/pr01a.htm#gtr00*.

ALABAMA

*Alabama State Law Library
300 Dexter Ave.
Montgomery, AL 36104
Phone: (334) 242-4347
Toll free: (800) 236-4069
E-mail: *reference@alalinc.net*
Web site: *www.alalinc.net/library/index.html*

*Bounds Law Library
University of Alabama
School of Law
P.O. Box 870383
Tuscaloosa, AL 35487-0383
Phone: (205) 348-5925
Fax: (205) 348-1112
E-mail: *cmiller@law.ua.edu*

*George H. Jones, Jr. Law Library
Thomas Goode School of Law
Faulkner University
5345 Atlanta Hwy.
Montgomery, AL 36109-3398
Phone: (334) 386-7210
Toll free: (800) 879-9816
Web site: *www.faulkner.edu/jones schooloflaw/library*

Jefferson County Law Library
2121 8th Ave., Ste. 500
Birmingham, AL 35203
Phone: (205) 325-5628
Fax: (205) 322-5915
Web site: *www.jclawlib.org*

Lucille Stewart Beeson Law Library
Cumberland School of Law
Samford University
800 Lakeshore Dr.
Birmingham, AL 35229
Phone: (205) 726-2714
Web site: *www.lawlib.samford.edu*

Montgomery County Law Library
Montgomery County Courthouse
251 S. Lawrence St.
Montgomery, AL 36104
Phone: (334) 832-1394
Fax: (334) 265-9536
E-mail: *teachduff@aol.com*
Web site: *http://15jc.alacourt.org/Law Library/about_the_law_library.htm*

ALASKA

*Alaska State Court Law Library
Anchorage Branch
303 K St.
Anchorage, AK 99501
Phone: (907) 264-0585
Fax: (907) 264-0733
Web site: *www.state.ak.us/courts/ libinfo.html*

Fairbanks Branch
Phone: (907) 452-9241

*Juneau Branch
Phone: (907) 463-4761

Ketchikan Branch
Phone: (907) 225-0500

ARIZONA

Arizona State Law Library
Arizona State Courts Bldg.
1501 W. Washington St., Ste. 102
Phoenix, AZ 85007
Phone: (602) 542-LAWS [5297]
Toll free: (800) 228-4710
(in AZ only)
E-mail: *sll@lib.az.us*
Web site: *www.dlapr.lib.az.us/law*

*James E. Rogers
College of Law Library
University of Arizona
1201 E. Speedway Blvd.
Tucson, AZ 85721
Phone: (520) 621-1413
Web site: *www.law.arizona.edu/ library*

*Ross-Blakley Law Library
Arizona State University
College of Law
McAllister & Orange Sts.
P.O. Box 877906
Tempe, AZ 85287-7906
Phone: (480) 965-6181
Web site: *www.law.asu.edu/library*

Pima County Law Library
110 W. Congress, Rm. 256
Tucson, AZ 85701-1317
Phone: (520) 740-8456
Fax: (520) 791-9122
E-mail: *pcll@sc.co.pima.az.us*
Web site: *www.sc.co.pima.az.us/lawlib*

Maricopa County Law Library
101 W. Jefferson
Phoenix, AZ 85003
Phone: (602) 506-3461
Fax: (602) 506-3677

Maricopa County Law Library
(second location)
222 E. Javelina
Mesa, AZ 85210
Phone: (602) 506-2065
Fax: (602) 506-2991
Web site: *www.superiorcourt.mari copa.gov/lawlibrary*

ARKANSAS

*Arkansas Supreme Court Library
Justice Bldg.
625 Marshall St., Ste. 1500
Little Rock, AR 72201
Phone: (501) 682-2147
Fax: (501) 682-6877
Web site: *http://courts.state.ar.us/ courts/sc_library.html*

*University of Arkansas at Little
Rock Pulaski County Law Library
1203 McMath Ave.
Little Rock, AR 72202
Phone: (501) 324-9444
Web site: *www.ualr.edu/~lawlib/ index.htm*

*Young Law Library
University of Arkansas
Waterman Hall
Fayetteville, AR 72701-1201
Phone: (479) 575-5051
Web site: *http://law-gopher.uark.edu/ library/library.html*

CALIFORNIA

*California Judicial Center Library
California Supreme Court
455 Golden Gate Ave., Rm. 4617
San Francisco, CA 94102-3660
Phone: (415) 865-7178

Alameda County Law Library
125 12th St.
Oakland, CA 94607-4912
Phone: (510) 208-4800
Fax: (510) 208-4836
Web site: *www.co.alameda.ca.us/law/ index.htm*

Chapman University
School of Law Library
1 University Dr.
Orange, CA 92866
Phone: (714) 628-2553
Web site: *www.chapman.edu/law/ library/f_index.html*

San Francisco Law Library
Civic Center (Main Library)
Veterans War Memorial Building
401 Van Ness Ave., Rm. 400
San Francisco, CA 94102
Phone: (415) 554-6821
Fax: (415) 554-6820

Financial District Branch
Monadnock Bldg.
685 Market St., Ste. 420
San Francisco, CA 94105
Phone: (415) 882-9310
Fax: (415) 882-9594

Courthouse Reference Room
Courthouse
400 McAllister St., Rm. 512
San Francisco, CA 94102
Phone: (415) 551-3647
Fax: (415) 551-3787
Web site: *www.sfgov.org/site/sfll_*
index.asp?id=4543

Contra Costa County
Public Law Library
Main Library
1020 Ward St.
Martinez, CA 94553
Phone: (925) 646-2783
Fax: (925) 646-2438

Richmond Branch
100 37th St., Rm. 237
Richmond, CA 94805
Phone: (510) 374-3019
Fax: (510) 374-3607
Web site: *www.cccpllib.org*

Elvin and Betty Wilson Library
University of La Verne
2040 3rd St.
La Verne, CA 91750
Phone: (909) 593-3511
Web site: *www.ulv.edu/~library/lib*
inf.htm

*Garrett W. McEnerny Law Library
at Boalt Hall
University of California, Berkeley
Boalt Hall
Berkeley, CA 94720-7200
Phone: (510) 642-0621
Fax: (510) 643-5039
Web site: *www.law.berkeley.edu/*
lawlibes/index.html

*Golden Gate University
Law Library
536 Mission St.
San Francisco, CA 94105
Phone: (415) 442-6680
Fax: (415) 512-9395
Web site:
http://internet.ggu.edu/law_library
**only access to federal depository
materials for general public**

*Gordon D. Schaber Law Library
University of the Pacific George
McGovern School of Law
3200 5th Ave.
Sacramento, CA 95817
Phone: (916) 739-7208
Web site: *www.mcgeorge.edu/*
campus_resources/library/index.htm
**only access to federal depository
materials for general public**

*Hastings College of Law Library
University of California, Hastings
200 McAllister St.
San Francisco, CA 94102
Phone: (415) 565-4750
Web site: *www.uchastings.edu/*
library/index.html

*Hugh and Hazel Darling
Law Library
UCLA School of Law
405 Hilgard Ave., Rm. 1112
Los Angeles, CA 90095-1458
Phone: (310) 825-4743
Web site:
www1.law.ucla.edu/~library
**must have proof of proper ID to
use library**

*Los Angeles County Law Library
301 W. 1st St.
Los Angeles, CA 90012
Phone: (213) 629-3531
Fax: (213) 613-1329
Web site: *http://lalaw.lib.ca.us*

Mendocino County Law Library
Mendocino County Courthouse
100 N. State St., Rm. 307
Ukiah, CA 95482
Phone: (707) 463-4201
Web site: *www.pacificsites.com/
~lawlib*

Monterey County Law Library
Monterey Location
Monterey Courthouse
1200 Aguajito Rd., Rm. 202
Monterey, CA 93940
Phone: (831) 647-7746
Fax: (831) 372-6036

Salinas Location
Federal Office Bldg.
100 W. Alisal, Ste. 144
Salinas, CA 93901
Phone: (831) 755-5046
Fax: (831) 422-9593
Web site: *http://fp.redshift.com/
mcolawlib*

*Orange County
Public Law Library
515 N. Flower St.
Santa Ana, CA 92703
Phone: (714) 834-3397
Web site: *www.oc.ca.gov/lawlib*

*San Diego County
Public Law Library
Main Library
1105 Front St.
San Diego, CA 92101-3904
Phone: (619) 531-3900
Fax: (619) 238-7716

North County Branch
325 S. Melrose Dr., Ste. 300
Vista, CA 92083-6697
Phone: (760) 940-4386
Fax: (760) 724-7694

South Bay Branch
500 3rd Ave.
Chula Vista, CA 91910-5617
Phone: (619) 691-4929
Fax: (619) 427-7521

East County Branch
250 E. Main St.
El Cajon, CA 92020-3941
Phone: (619) 441-4451
Fax: (619) 441-0235
Web site: *www.sdcll.org/index.html*

San Mateo County Law Library
Cohn-Sorenson Law Library
710 Hamilton St.
Redwood City, CA 94063
Phone: (650) 363-4913
Web site: *www.smcll.org*

Santa Barbara County Law Library
1100 Anacapa
Santa Barbara, CA 93101
Phone: (805) 568-2296
Fax: (805) 568-2299
Web site: *www.countylawlibrary.org*

Santa Maria Law Library (Branch of
Santa Barbara County Law Library)
312 E. Cook St.
Santa Maria, CA 93454
Phone: (805) 346-7548
Fax: (805) 346-7692
Web site:
*www.countylawlibrary.org/santa
maria.htm*

Santa Clara County Law Library
360 N. 1st St.
San Jose, CA 95113
Phone: (408) 299-3567
Web site: *www.sccll.org*

Santa Cruz County Law Library
County Government Center
701 Ocean St., Rm. 070
Santa Cruz, CA 95060-4003
Phone: (831) 457-2525
Web site: *www.lawlibrary.org/
index.html*

Sonoma County Law Library
600 Administration Dr., Rm. 213-J
Santa Rosa, CA 95403
Phone: (707) 565-2668
Fax: (707) 565-1126
Web site: *www.sonomacounty
lawlibrary.org*

Thomas Jefferson
School of Law Library
2121 San Diego Ave.
San Diego, CA 92110
Phone: (619) 297-9700
Web site:
www.jeffersonlaw.edu/index.cfm

*University of California, Davis
Law Library
400 Mrak Hall Dr.
Davis, CA 95616
Phone: (530) 752-3327
Fax: (530) 752-8766
Web site:
http://lawlibrary.ucdavis.edu

*Dorraine Zief Law Library
University of San Francisco
Law School
2131 Fulton St.
San Francisco, CA 94117-1080
Phone: (415) 422-6679
Fax: (415) 422-2345
Web site: *www.usfca.edu/law_library*
**only access to federal depository
materials for general public**

USC Law Library
699 Exposition Rd., Rm. 202
Los Angeles, CA 90089
Phone: (213) 740-6482
Web site: *http://lawweb.usc.edu/
library/*

*Whittier Law School Law Library
3333 Harbor Rd.
Costa Mesa, CA 92626
Phone: (714) 444-4141
Web site:
*www.law.whittier.edu/library/library
facility.asp*
**only access to federal depository
materials for general public**

*William M. Rains Law Library
Loyola Law School
919 S. Albany
Los Angeles, CA 90015-1211
Phone: (213) 736-1177
Web site:
www.lls.edu/library/index.html
**only access to federal depository
materials for general public; call
ahead**

COLORADO

*Colorado Supreme Court
Law Library
B112 State Judicial Bldg.
2 E. 14th Ave.
Denver, CO 80203
Phone: (303) 837-3720
Web site: *www.state.co.us/courts/
sctlib*

*University of Colorado
Law Library
2405 Kittredge Loop Dr.
Boulder, CO 80309-0402
Phone: (303) 492-7534
Web site: *www.colorado.edu/law/
lawlib*

*Westminster Law Library
University of Denver Law School
1900 Olive St.
Denver, CO 80220
Phone: (303) 871-6190
Fax: (303) 871-6999
Web site: *www.law.du.edu/library/
default.htm*
**only access to federal depository
materials for general public**

CONNECTICUT

Connecticut Judicial
Branch Libraries
Law Library at
Bridgeport Courthouse
1061 Main St.
Bridgeport, CT 06604
Phone: (203) 579-6237
Fax: (203) 579-6512

Law Library at
Danbury Courthouse
146 White St.
Danbury, CT 06810
Phone: (203) 207-8625
Fax: (203) 207-8627

Law Library at
Hartford Courthouse
95 Washington St.
Hartford, CT 06106
Phone: (860) 548-2866
Fax: (860) 548-2868

Law Library at
Litchfield Courthouse
15 West St.
Litchfield, CT 06759
Phone: (860) 567-0598
Fax: (860) 567-4533

Law Library at
Middletown Courthouse
1 Court St.
Middletown, CT 06457
Phone: (860) 343-6560
Fax: (860) 343-6568

Law Library at
New Britain Courthouse
20 Franklin Sq.
New Britain, CT 06051
Phone: (860) 515-5110
Fax: (860) 515-5111

Law Library at
New Haven Courthouse
235 Church St.
New Haven, CT 06510
Phone: (203) 503-6828
Fax: (203) 789-6499

Law Library at
New London Courthouse
70 Huntington St.
New London, CT 06320
Phone: (860) 442-7561
Fax: (860) 442-9416

Law Library at
Norwich Courthouse
1 Courthouse Sq.
Norwich, CT 06360
Phone: (860) 887-2398
Fax: (860) 823-1752

Law Library at
Putnam Courthouse
155 Church St.
Putnam, CT 06260
Phone: (860) 928-3716
Fax: (860) 963-7531

Law Library at
Rockville Courthouse
69 Brooklyn St.
Rockville, CT 06066
Phone: (860) 896-4955
Fax: (860) 875-3213

Law Library at
Stamford Courthouse
123 Hoyt St.
Stamford, CT 06905
Phone: (203) 965-5250
Fax: (203) 965-5784

Law Library at
Waterbury Courthouse
300 Grand St.
Waterbury, CT 06702
Phone: (203) 591-3338
Fax: (203) 596-4317

Law Library at
Willimantic Courthouse
108 Valley St.
Willimantic, CT 06226
Phone: (860) 450-0627
Fax: (860) 423-0772

Web site for all libraries:
www.jud.state.ct.us/lawlib

*Connecticut State Library
231 Capitol Ave.
Hartford, CT 06106
Phone: (860) 757-6500
Web site: *www.cslib.org/isd.htm*

*Lillian Goldman Law Library
Yale Law School
127 Wall St.
New Haven, CT 06520-8215
Phone: (203) 432-1606
call ahead

*University of Connecticut
School of Law Library
39 Elizabeth St.
Hartford, CT 06105
Phone: (860) 570-5200
Web site: *www.law.uconn.edu/library*

DELAWARE

*Legal Information Center
Widener University
School of Law Library
4601 Concord Pike
Wilmington, DE 19803
Phone: (302) 477-2114
Web site: *www.law.widener.edu/
law-library*

FLORIDA

Barry University
Law School Library
6441 E. Colonial Dr.
Orlando, FL 32807
Phone: (407) 275-2000
Fax: (407) 275-2010
Web site: *www.barry.edu/law/library/
default.asp*

*Broward County Law Library
100 S. Andrews Ave.
Ft. Lauderdale, FL 33301
Phone: (954) 357-7444
Web site: *www.broward.org/
bclblg.htm*

Library and Technology Center
Florida Coastal School of Law
7555 Beach Blvd.
Jacksonville, FL 32216
Phone: (904) 680-7700
Web site: *www.fcsl.edu/library/
information/frameset.html*

*Florida State University
College of Law Library
425 W. Jefferson St.
Tallahassee, FL 32306-1600
Phone: (850) 644-3400
Web site: *www.law.fsu.edu/library*

Florida Supreme Court Law Library
500 S. Duval St.
Tallahassee, FL 32399-6556
Phone: (850) 488-8919
Web site: *http://library.flcourts.org*

Hernando County Law Library
Hernando County Courthouse
20 N. Main St.
Brooksville, FL 34601
Phone: (352) 540-6248
Web site:
www.clerk.co.hernando.fl.us/other/
lawlibrary.html

Lake County Law Library
202 N. Sinclair Ave.
Tavares, FL 32778
Phone: (352) 742-4161
Web site: *www.lakecountyclerk.org/*
services.asp?subject=law_library

*Legal Information Center
University of Florida
Levin College of Law
25th St. & S.W. 2nd Ave.
P.O. Box 117628
Gainesville, FL 32611-7628
Phone: (352) 392-0417
Fax: (352) 392-5093
Web site: *www.law.ufl.edu/lic*

Manatee County Law Library
1115 Manatee Ave., West
Bradenton, FL 34206
Phone: (941) 741-4090
Fax: (941) 741-4085
Web site:
www.clerkofcourts.com/courtservices/
lawlib/library.htm

*Nova Southeastern University
Shepard Broad Law Center
3305 College Ave.
Ft. Lauderdale, FL 33314
Phone: (954) 262-6202
Web site: *www.nsulaw.nova.edu/*
library/index.cfm

Polk County Law Library
225 N. Broadway, Rm. 3076
Bartow, FL 33830
Phone: (863) 534-4013
Web site: *www.pclc.lib.fl.us/*
lawlib.htm

St. Thomas University
Law School Library
16400 N.W. 32nd Ave.
Miami, FL 33054
Phone: (305) 623-2331
Web site: *www.stu.edu/lawlib*

*Stetson University
College of Law Library
1401 61st St., South
Gulfport, FL 33707-3299
Phone: (727) 562-7800
Web site: *www.law.stetson.edu/lawlib*

University of Miami
School of Law Library
1311 Miller Dr.
Coral Gables, FL 33146
Phone: (305) 284-3563
Web site:
http://library.law.miami.edu/
spublic.html

Volusia County Law Library
Volusia County Courthouse
101 N. Alabama Ave., Rm. B318
DeLand, Florida 32724
Phone: (386) 822-5769
Fax: (386) 943-7018

*Volusia County Courthouse Annex
125 E. Orange Ave., Rm. 208
Daytona Beach, FL 32114
Phone: (386) 257-6041
Fax: (386) 257-6052

New Smyrna Beach Public Library
1001 S. Dixie Frwy.
New Smyrna Beach, FL 32168
Phone: (386) 257-6041
Web site: *www.vclawlib.org*

GEORGIA

Fulton County Law Library
185 Central Ave., SW
Atlanta, GA 30303
Phone: (404) 730-4544
Fax: (404) 730-4565
Web site: *http://fultoncourt.org/
lawlibrary/index.html*

*Furman Smith Law Library
Mercer University Law School
1021 Georgia Ave.
Macon, Georgia 31207-0001
Phone: (478) 301-2612
Fax: (478) 301-2284
Web site: *http://library.law.mercer.edu*

*Georgia State University
College of Law Library
140 Decatur St., SE
Atlanta, GA 30303
Phone: (404) 651-2479
Web site: *http://law.gsu.edu/
lawlibrary/index.htm*

Gwinnett County Law Library
75 Langley Dr.
Lawrenceville, GA 30045
Phone: (770) 822-8577
Fax: (770) 822-8570
Web site: *www.gcll.org*

Alexander Campbell King
Law Library
University of Georgia School of Law
Herty Dr.
Athens, GA 30602
Phone: (706) 542-8480
Web site: *www.law.uga.edu/library*

HAWAII

*Administrative Offices of the
Courts Law Library
Ali'iolani Hale
417 S. King St.
Honolulu, HI 96813-2902
Phone: (808) 539-4964

Maui 2nd Judicial Circuit Law
Library
Hoapili Hale
2145 Main St.
Wailuku, HI 96793-1679
Phone: (808) 244-2959

Hawai'i 3rd Judicial Circuit
Law Library
75 Aupuni St.
Hilo, HI 96720-4253
Phone: (808) 961-7438

Kaua'i 5th Judicial Circuit
Law Library
3059 Umi St.
Lihu'e, HI 96766-1809
Phone: (808) 246-3327
Web site for above libraries:
*www.courts.State.hi.us/page_server/
Home/6267457137944F4CE96F55
5610.html*

*William S. Richardson
School of Law Library
University of Hawaii, Manoa
2525 Dole St.
Honolulu, HI 96822
Phone: (808) 956-7583
Web site: *http://library.law.hawaii.
edu/index.html*

IDAHO

*Idaho State Law Library
Supreme Court Bldg.
451 W. State St.
Boise, ID 83720-0051
Phone: (208) 334-3316
Fax: (208) 334-4019
Web site: *www2.state.id.us/lawlib/
lawlib.html*

University of Idaho Law Library
6th & Rayburn St.
Moscow, ID 83844-2324
Phone: (208) 885-6521
Fax: (208) 885-2743
Web site: *www.law.uidaho.edu/
library/default.asp*

ILLINOIS

*Albert E. Jenner Memorial Library
University of Illinois at Urbana
Champaign Law School
142 Law Bldg.
504 E. Pennsylvania Ave.
Champaign, IL 61820
Phone: (217) 333-2914
Web site: *http://library.law.uiuc.edu*

*Chicago-Kent Law Library
Downtown Campus of Illinois
Institute of Technology
565 W. Adams St.
Chicago, IL 60661
Phone: (312) 906-5600
Web site: *http://library.kentlaw.edu*

*D'Angelo Law Library
University of Chicago Law School
1121 E. 60th St.
Chicago, IL 60637-2745
Phone: (773) 702-9613
Web site: *www.lib.uchicago.edu/e/
law/using*
**only access to federal depository
materials for general public; call
ahead**

*David C. Shapiro Memorial
Law Library
Northern Illinois University
College of Law
Swen Parson Hall, Rm. 276
DeKalb, Il 60115
Phone: (815) 753-0507
Web site: *www3.niu.edu/claw/
library/library2.htm*

*John Marshall
School of Law Library
315 S. Plymouth Ct.
Chicago, IL 60604
Phone: (312) 427-2737, ext. 729
Web site: *www.jmls.edu/catalog.cfm?
dest.=dir&linkon=section&linkid=23*
call ahead

*Loyola University Chicago
School of Law Library
25 E. Pearson St.
Chicago, IL 60611
Phone: (312) 915-7200
Web site: *www.luc.edu/libraries/law*
**only access to federal depository
materials for general public; call
ahead**

*Pritzker Legal Research Center
Northwestern University
School of Law
357 E. Chicago Ave.
Chicago, IL 60611
Phone: (312) 503-8451
Fax: (312) 503-9230
Web site: *www.law.nwu.edu/
lawlibrary*

*Southern Illinois University
School of Law Library
Lesar Law Bldg.
Carbondale, IL 62901
Phone: (618) 453-8796
Web site: *www.law.siu.edu/lawlib/
index.htm*

*Vincent G. Rinn Law Library
DePaul University
College of Law Library
25 E. Jackson
Chicago, IL 60604
Phone: (312) 362-8121
Web site: *http://www.law.depaul.
edu/library_resources/library/*

INDIANA

*Ruth Lilly Law Library
Indiana University School of Law,
Indianapolis
530 W. New York St.
Indianapolis, IN 46202-3225
Phone: (317) 274-4028
Web site: *www.iulaw.indy.indiana.
edu/library/library.htm*

*Indiana University School of Law
Library, Bloomington
211 S. Indiana Ave.
Bloomington, IN 47405-7001
Phone: (812) 855-9666
Web site: *www.law.indiana.edu/
lib/index.html*

*Kresge Law Library
University of Notre Dame
Law School
Notre Dame, IN 46556
Phone: (574) 631-7024
Fax: (574) 631-6371
Web site: *www.nd.edu/~lawlib*

*Valparaiso Law School Library
656 S. Greenwich St.
Valparaiso, IN 46383
Phone: (219) 465-7827
Fax: (219) 465-7917
Web site: *www.valpo.edu/law/library*

IOWA

*Drake Law Library
2507 University Ave.
Des Moines, IA 50311-4505
Phone: (515) 271-2824
Web site: *www.law.drake.edu/library*

State Library of Iowa
Historical Building (Capitol)
E. 12th St. & Grand Ave.
Des Moines, IA 50319-0001
Phone: (515) 281-5124
Web site: *www.silo.lib.ia.us/
specialized-services/law-library/
index.html*

University of Iowa Law Library
200 Boyd Law Bldg.
Iowa City, IA 52242-1166
Phone: (319) 335-9104
Fax: (319) 335-9039
Web site: *www.uiowa.edu/~lawlib/
policies.html*

KANSAS

*Kansas Supreme Court
Law Library
301 W. 10th
Topeka, KS 66612
Phone: (785) 296-3257
Fax: (785) 296-1863
Web site: *www.kscourts.org/ctlib*

*Wheat Law Library
University of Kansas Law School
Green Hall
1535 W. 15th St.
Lawrence, KS 66045
Phone: (785) 864-3025
Web site: *www.law.ukans.edu/library*

*Washburn University
School of Law Library
1700 S.W. College
Topeka, KS 66621
Phone: (785) 231-1088
Fax: (785) 231-1087
Web site: *washburnlaw.edu/library*

KENTUCKY

Jefferson County
Public Law Library
514 W. Liberty St., Ste. 240
Old Jail Bldg.
Louisville, KY 40202-2806
Phone: (502) 574-5943
Fax: (502) 574-3483
Web site: *www.jcpll.com*

*Salmon P. Chase
College of Law Library
Northern Kentucky University
Nunn Dr.
Highland Heights, KY 41099-6110
Phone: (859) 572-5456
Web site: *www.nku.edu/~chase/
library/lib_home.htm*

*University of Kentucky
Law Library
620 S. Limestone St.
Lexington, KY 40506-0048
Phone: (859) 257-8686
Web site: *www.uky.edu/law/library*

University of Louisville
School of Law Library
2301 S. 3rd St.
Lexington KY 40292-0001
Phone: (502) 852-6392
Fax: (502) 852-8906
Web site: *www.louisville.edu/
library/law*

LOUISIANA

*Louisiana State Law Library
301 Loyola Ave.
New Orleans, LA 70112
Phone: (504) 568-5705
Web site: *www.lasc.org/law_lib
&legal_res/index.asp*

Paul M. Herbert Law Center
Louisiana State University
Law School
1 E. Campus Dr.
Baton Rouge, LA 70803-1010
Phone: (225) 578-8802
Fax: (225) 578-5773
Web site: *www.law.lsu.edu/library/
f_lib01.ht*m

*Loyola University
School of Law Library
7214 St. Charles Ave.
New Orleans, LA 70118
Phone: (504) 861-5545
Web site: *http://law.loyno.edu/library/
index.html*

*Tulane University
School of Law Library
6329 Freret St.
New Orleans, LA 70118-6231
Phone: (504) 865-5952
Web site: *www.law.tulane.edu/
tuexp/index.cfm?d=library&main=
libguide.htm*

MAINE

*Donald L. Garbrecht Law Library
246 Deering Ave.
Portland, ME 04102-2898
Phone: (207) 780-4351
Web site: *http://mainelaw.maine.
edu/library1.htm*

Nathan and Henry B. Cleaves
Law Library
142 Federal St.
Portland, ME 04101
Phone: (207) 773-9712
Fax: (207) 773-2155
Web site: *www.cleaves.org*

*Maine State Law and Legislative
Reference Library
43 State House Station
Augusta, ME 04333-0043
Phone: (207) 287-1600
Web site: *www.state.me.us/legis/
lawlib/homepage.htm*

MARYLAND

Maryland State Law Library
Robert C. Murphy
Courts of Appeal Bldg.
361 Rowe Blvd.
Annapolis, MD 21401-1697
Phone: (410) 260-1430
Fax: (410) 974-2063
Web site: *www.lawlib.state.md.us*

*University of Baltimore
School of Law Library
1415 Maryland Ave.
Baltimore, MD 21201
Phone: (410) 837-4554
Fax: (410) 837-4570
Web site: *http://law.ubalt.edu/lawlib/
index.html*

MASSACHUSETTS

*Boston College Law Library
885 Centre St.
Newton Centre, MA 02459
Phone: (617) 552-4407
Web site: *http://infoeagle.bc.edu/
schools/law/library*
call ahead

Pappas Law Library
Boston University Law School
765 Commonwealth Ave.
Boston, MA 02215
Phone: (617) 552-4407
Web site: *www.bu.edu/lawlibrary*

*Harvard Law School Library
1545 Massachusetts Ave.
Cambridge, MA 02138
Phone: (617) 495-3455
Web site: *www.law.harvard.edu/
library/circ/circ_access_dept.htm*
call ahead

Massachusetts Trial Court
Law Libraries
Barnstable Law Library
1st District Courthouse
Barnstable, MA 02630
Phone: (508) 362-8539
Fax: (508) 362-1374

Brockton Law Library
Superior Courthouse
72 Belmont St.
Brockton, MA 02301
Phone: (508) 586-7110
Fax: (508) 588-8483

Middlesex Law Library
Superior Courthouse
40 Thorndike St.
Cambridge, MA 02141
Phone: (617) 494-4148
Fax: (617) 225-0026

Fall River Law Library
Superior Courthouse
441 N. Main St.
Fall River, MA 02720
Phone: (508) 676-8971
Fax: (508) 677-2966

Fitchburg Law Library
Superior Courthouse
84 Elm St.
Fitchburg, MA 01420
Phone: (978) 345-6726
Fax: (978) 345-7334

Franklin Law Library
Courthouse
425 Main St.
Greenfield, MA 01301
Phone: (413) 772-6580
Fax: (413) 772-0743

Lawrence Law Library
2 Appleton St.
Lawrence, MA 01840
Phone: (978) 687-7608
Fax: (978) 688-2346

Lowell Law Library
Superior Courthouse
360 Gorham St.
Lowell, MA 01852
Phone: (978) 452-9301
Fax: (978) 970-2000

New Bedford Law Library
Superior Courthouse
441 County St.
New Bedford, MA 02740
Phone: (508) 992-8077
Fax: (508) 991-7411

Plymouth Law Library
County Commissioners' Bldg.
11 S. Russell St.
Plymouth, MA 02360
Phone: (508) 747-4796
Fax: (508) 746-9788

Essex Law Library
Superior Courthouse
34 Federal St.
Salem, MA 01970
Phone: (978) 741-0674
Fax: (978) 745-7224

*Hampden Law Library
Courthouse
50 State St.
Springfield, MA 01101
Phone: (413) 748-7923
Fax: (413) 734-2973

Bristol Law Library
Superior Courthouse
9 Court St.
Taunton, MA 02780
Phone: (508) 824-7632
Fax: (508) 824-4723

Worcester Law Library
Courthouse
2 Main St.
Worcester, MA 01608
Phone: (508) 770-1899
Fax: (508) 754-9933
Web site: *www.lawlib.state.ma.us/*
index.htm

Northeastern University
School of Law Library
400 Huntington Ave.
Boston, MA 02115
Phone: (617) 373-3332
Web site: *www.slaw.neu.edu/library/*
default.htm

*Social Law Library
Supreme Judicial Court
1 Pemberton Sq., Ste. 1200
Boston, MA 02108-1792
Phone: (617) 523-0018, ext. 520

Southern New England
School of Law Library
333 Union St.
New Bedford, MA 02740
Phone: (508) 998-9888, ext. 121
Web site: *www.snesl.edu/library.htm*

MICHIGAN

Oakland County Law Library
1200 N. Telegraph Rd.
Pontiac, MI 48341
Phone: (248) 858-0012
Fax: (248) 452-9145
Web site: *www.co.oakland.mi.us/*
lawlib

*Arthur Neef Law Library
Wayne State University Law School
474 Ferry Mall
Detroit, MI 48202
Phone: (313) 577-3925
Fax: (313) 577-5498
Web site: *www.lib.wayne.edu/*
lawlibrary

Ave Maria School of Law Library
3475 Plymouth Rd.
Ann Arbor, MI 48105-2550
Phone: (734) 827-8040
Web site: *www.avemarialaw.edu/*
library/lawlib7.cfm

Grand Traverse County Law Library
328 Washington St.
Traverse City, MI 49684
Phone: (231) 922-4715
Fax: (231) 922-4519
Web site: *http://tadl.tcnet.org/index/*
lawlib.htm

*Kresge Law Library
University of Detroit Mercy
School of Law
651 E. Jefferson
Detroit, MI 48226
Phone: (313) 596-0200
Web site: *www.law.udmercy.edu/*
currentstudents/kresge
**only access to federal depository
materials for general public; call
ahead**

Library of Michigan Law Library
525 W. Ottawa
Lansing, MI 48933
Phone: (517) 373-0630
Fax: (517) 373-3915
Web site: *www.michigan.gov/hal/0,
1607,7-160-17449_18639---,00.html*

Dickinson County Law Library
401 Iron Mountain St.
Iron Mountain, MI 49801-3435
Phone: (906) 774-1218
Fax: (906) 774-4079
Web site: *www.dcl-lib.org*

Escanaba Public Library
400 Ludington St.
Escanaba, MI 49829-3924
Phone: (906) 789-7323
Fax: (906) 786-0942
Web site: *www.uproc.lib.mi.us/epl*

*Kenneth J. Shouldice Library
Lake Superior State University
906 Ryan St.
Sault Ste. Marie, MI 49783-1632
Phone: (906) 635-2815
Fax: (906) 635-2167
Web site: *www.lssu.edu/library*

*Lydia M. Olson Library
Northern Michigan University
1401 Presque Isle Ave.
Marquette, MI 49855-5376
Phone: (906) 227-2260
Fax: (906) 227-1333
Web site: *www.nmu.edu/www-sam/
ais/index.htm*

Alpena County Law Library
Alpena County Courthouse
720 W. Chisholm, Ste. 1
Alpena, MI 49707-2453
Phone: (989) 356-0395
Fax: (989) 354-3748

Finch Library Law Collection
Central Michigan University
300 E. Preston St.
Mt. Pleasant, MI 48859-0001
Phone: (989) 774-3470
Fax: (989) 774-4499
Web site: *www.lib.cmich.edu*

Library for Information,
Technology and Education
Ferris State University
1010 Campus Dr.
Big Rapids, MI 49307
Phone: (231) 591-3730
Fax: (231) 591-2662
Web site: *http://library.ferris.edu*

Kirtland Community
College Law Library
10775 N. St., Helen Rd.
Roscommon, MI 48653-9634
Phone: (989) 275-5121, ext. 246
Fax: (989) 275-8510
Web site:
www.kirtland.cc.mi.us/library

*Osterlin Library
Northwestern Michigan College
1701 S. Front St.
Traverse City, MI 49686-3061
Phone: (231) 922-1540
Fax: (231) 922-1056
Web site: *www.nmc.edu/library*

Ann Arbor District Library
343 S. 5th Ave.
Ann Arbor, MI 48104-2293
Phone: (734) 327-4266
Fax: (734) 327-8307
Web site: *www.aadl.org*

Henry Ford Centennial Library
16301 Michigan Ave.
Dearborn, MI 48126-2792
Phone: (313) 943-2330
Fax: (313) 943-2853
Web site: *http://dearborn.lib.mi.us*

Detroit Public Library
Sociology & Economics Section
5201 Woodward Ave.
Detroit, MI 48202
Phone: (313) 833-1440
Fax: (313) 833-1442
Web site: *www.detroit.lib.mi.us/se*

*Bruce T. Halle Library
Eastern Michigan University
955 W. Circle Dr.
Ypsilanti, MI 48197
Phone: (734) 487-0020, ext. 2100
Fax: (734) 487-8861
Web site: *www.emich.edu/halle*

Farmington Community Library
32737 W. Twelve Mile Rd.
Farmington Hills, MI 48334-3302
Phone: (248) 553-0300
Fax: (248) 553-3228
Web site: *www.farmlib.org*

Genesee County Law Library
900 S. Saginaw
Flint, MI 48502
Phone: (810) 257-4463
Fax: (810) 239-9280
Web site: *www.co.genesee.mi.us*

Genesee District Library
4195 W. Pasadena Ave.
Flint, MI 48504-2375
Phone: (810) 732-5570
Fax: (810) 732-1161
Web site: *http://gdl.falcon.edu*

Eschleman Library
Henry Ford Community College
5101 Evergreen Rd.
Dearborn, MI 48120
Phone: (313) 845-6375
Fax: (313) 271-5868

Macomb County Library
16480 Hall Road
Clinton Township, MI 48038-1140
Phone: (586) 286-6660
Fax: (586) 412-5958
Web site: *www.libcoop.net/mcl*

*Monroe County Library System
3700 S. Custer Rd.
Monroe, MI 48161-9732
Phone: (734) 241-5277
Fax: (734) 241-4722
Web site: *www.monroe.lib.mi.us*

*St. Clair County
Community Library
Port Huron Main Branch
210 McMorran Blvd.
Port Huron, MI 48060
Phone: (810) 987-7323
Fax: (810) 987-7874
Web site: *www.sccl.lib.mi.us*

University of Michigan Law Library
801 Monroe St.
Ann Arbor, MI 48109-1210
Phone: (734) 764-9324
Fax: (734) 615-0178
Web site: *www.law.umich.edu/library*

*Warren Public Library
Arthur J. Miller Branch
4700 E. 13 Mile Rd.
Warren, MI 48092
Phone: (810) 751-5377
Fax: (810) 751-5902
Web site: *www.libcoop.net/warren*

Learning Resource Center
Washtenaw Community College
4800 Huron River Dr.
Ann Arbor, MI 48106
Phone: (734) 973-3300
Fax: (734) 677-2220
Web site: *www.wccnet.org/library*

*Delta College Library
1961 Delta Rd.
University Center, MI 48710-0001
Phone: (989) 686-9000
Fax: (989) 686-4131
Web site: *www.delta.edu/library*

*Hoyt Public Library
505 Jane St.
Saginaw, MI 48607
Phone: (989) 755-0994
Fax: (989) 755-9829
Web site: *www.saginaw.lib.mi.us*

Jackson District Library
Carnegie Branch
244 W. Michigan Ave.
Jackson, MI 49201-2275
Phone: (517) 788-44087, ext. 234
Fax: (517) 788-6024
Web site: *www.jackson.lib.mi.us*

Lenawee County Library
4459 W. US 223
Adrian, MI 49221-9461
Phone: (517) 263-1011
Fax: (517) 263-7109
Web site: *www.lenawee.lib.mi.us*

Livingston County Law Library
Judicial Center Bldg., Ste. 5
204 S. Highlander Way
Howell, MI 48843
Phone: (517) 546-8079
Fax: (517) 546-0048
Web site: *http://co.livingston.mi.us/
circuitcourtadmin/law_library.htm*

College of Law Library
Michigan State University, Detroit
368 Law College Bldg.
E. Lansing, MI 48824
Phone: (517) 432-6870
Fax: (517) 432-6861
Web site: *www.dcl.edu/library/
index.html*

Michigan State University Library
100 Library
East Lansing, MI 48824-1048
Phone: (517) 353-8700
Fax: (517) 432-8050
Web site: *www.lib.msu.edu*

Hoyt Main Public Library
Public Libraries of Saginaw
505 Janes St.
Saginaw, MI 48607
Phone: (989) 755-0904
Fax: (989) 755-9829
Web site: *www.saginaw.lib.mi.us*

Saginaw County Law Library
Saginaw Courthouse, LL 007
111 S. Michigan Ave.
Saginaw, MI 48602
Phone: (989) 790-5533
Fax: (989) 793-8180

*Thomas M. Cooley Law Library
334 S. Washington Ave.
Lansing, MI 48901
Phone: (517) 371-5140, ext. 3111
Fax: (517) 334-5715
Web site: *www.cooley.edu/library/
index.htm*

Grand Rapids Public Library
1100 Hynes Ave., Southwest, Ste. B
Grand Rapids, MI 49507
Phone: (616) 988-5400
Fax: (616) 988-5419
Web site: *www.grpl.org*

Steelcase Library/De Vos Center
Grand Valley State University
401 W. Fulton
Grand Rapids, MI 49501
Phone: (616) 336-7338
Fax: (616) 336-7340
Web site: *www.gvsu.edu/library*

*Hackley Public Library
316 W. Webster Ave.
Muskegon, MI 49440-1281
Phone: (231) 722-7276
Fax: (231) 726-5567
Web site: *www.hackleylibrary.org*

Kalamazoo County Law Library
315 S. Rose St.
Kalamazoo, MI 49007
Phone: (269) 553-7920, Law Desk
Fax: (269) 342-8324
Web site: *www.kpl.gov*

Kent District Library
Plainfield Branch
2650 Five Mile Northeast
Grand Rapids, MI 49525
Phone: (616) 647-3930
Fax: (616) 361-1007
Web site: *www.kdl.org/branches/
plainfield.html*

Niles Community Library
620 E. Main St.
Niles, MI 49120-2620
Phone: (616) 683-8545, ext. 3315
Fax: (616) 683-0075
Web site: *www.nileslibrary.com*

MINNESOTA

*Minnesota State Law Library
Minnesota Judicial Center, Rm. G25
25 Rev. Dr. Martin Luther King, Jr.
Blvd.
St. Paul, MN 55155
Phone: (651) 296-2775
Fax: (651) 296-6740
Web site: *www.lawlibrary.state.mn.us*

Washington County Law Library
Government Center, Rm. 150
14949 62nd St. North
Stillwater, MN 55082
Phone: (651) 430-6330
Web site: *www.washcolaw.lib.mn.us*

Clay County Law Library
Clay County Courthouse
807 11th St. North
Moorhead, MN 56560
Phone: (218) 299-7522
Fax: (218) 299-5237
Web site: *www.mnstate.edu/govdocs/
legal2.htm*

Dakota County Law Library
1560 Highway 55
Hastings, MN 55033
Phone: (651) 438-8080
Fax: (651) 438-8098
Web site: *www.co.dakota.mn.us/
law_lib/index.htm*

Hennepin County Law Library
C-2451 Government Center
300 S. 6th St.
Minneapolis, MN 55487
Phone: (612) 348-2903
Fax: (612) 348-2372
Web site: *http://hclaw.co.hennepin.
mn.us*

*University of Minnesota
Law Library
Walter F. Mondale Hall
229 19th Ave. South
Minneapolis, MN 55455
Phone: (612) 625-4300
Fax: (612) 625-3478
Web site: *www.law.umn.edu/library/
home.html*

Warren E. Burger Law Library
William Mitchell College of Law
875 Summit Ave.
St. Paul, MN 55105-3076
Phone: (651) 227-9171
Web site: *www.wmitchell.edu/library/
index.html*

MISSISSIPPI

*Mississippi Supreme Court Library
450 High St.
Jackson, MS 39201-1083
Phone: (601) 359-3672
Web site: *www.mssc.state.ms.us/
library/default.asp*

*James O. Eastland Law Library
1 Grove Loop
University, MS 38677-1848
Phone: (662) 915-6824
Web site: *http://library.law.ole miss.edu*

MISSOURI

*Leon E. Bloch Law Library
5100 Rockhill Rd.
Kansas City, MO 64110-2499
Phone: (816) 235-1650
Web site: *www1.law.umkc.edu/ library*

*Omer Poos Law Library
St. Louis University Law School
3700 Lindell Blvd.
St. Louis, MO 63108
Phone: (314) 977-3081
Web site: *http://lawlib.slu.edu/library*

Columbia School of Law Library
University of Missouri
226 Hulston Hall
Columbia, MO 65211-4190
Phone: (573) 882-1123
Fax: (573) 882-9676
Web site: *www.law.missouri.edu/ library*

*Washington University
Law Library
Anheuser Busch Hall
1 Brookings Dr.
St. Louis, MO 63130-4899
Phone: (314) 935-6450
Web site: *www.wulaw.wustl.edu/ Infores/library/*

MONTANA

*State Law Library of Montana
Justice Building
215 N. Sanders
Helena, MT 59620-3004
Phone: (406) 444-3660
Fax: (406) 444-3603
Web site: *www.lawlibrary.state.mt.us*

William T. Jameson Law Library
University of Montana
School of Law
6th St. & Maurice
Missoula, MT 59812-9936
Phone: (406) 243-6171
Web site: *www.umt.edu/law/library/ library.htm*

NEBRASKA

*Klutznick Law Library
Creighton University
2500 California Plaza
Omaha, NE 68178-0340
Phone: (402) 280-5541
Fax: (402) 280-2244
Web site: *http://culaw2.creighton.edu/ library/index.html*

*University of Nebraska, Lincoln
Schmid Law Library
Ross McCollum Hall
40th & Fair Sts.
Lincoln, NE 68583-0902
Phone: (402) 472-3547
Fax: (402) 472-8260
Web site: *www.unl.edu/lawcoll/ schmid/index.html*

*Nebraska Supreme Court
Nebraska State Library
P.O. Box 98910
State Capitol Bldg.
15th & K Sts.
Lincoln, NE 68509-8931
Phone: (402) 471-3189
Fax: (402) 471-1011
Web site: *http://court.nol.org/
library/lawlibindex.htm*

NEVADA

*Nevada Supreme Court
Law Library
Capitol Complex, No. 100
201 S. Carson St.
Carson City, NV 89701-4702
Phone: (775) 684-1640
Fax: (775) 684-1662
Web site: *www.clan.lib.nv.us/polpac/
library/clan/nscl.htm*

*University of Nevada, Las Vegas
William S. Boyd
School of Law Library
4505 Maryland Pkwy.
P.O. Box 451003
Las Vegas, NV 89154-1003
Phone: (702) 895-2440
Fax: (702) 895-2414
Web site: *www.law.unlv.edu/
library.html*

*Washoe County Law Library
Courthouse, Rm. 101
75 Court St.
Reno, NV 89501
Phone: (775) 328-3250
Fax: (775) 328-3441
Web site: *http://207.228.25.168/lawlib*

NEW HAMPSHIRE

*Franklin Pierce Law Center Library
2 White St.
Concord, NH 03301-4197
Phone: (603) 228-1541
Fax: (603) 228-0388
Web site:
www.fplc.edu/library/library.htm
** only access to federal depository
materials for general public**

*New Hampshire Supreme Court
New Hampshire Law Library
1 Noble Dr.
Concord, NH 03301-6160
Phone: (603) 271-3777
Fax: (603) 271-2168
Web site: *www.courts.state.nh.us/
lawlibrary/index.htm*

NEW JERSEY

*New Jersey State Library
P.O. Box 520
185 W. State St.
Trenton, NJ 08625-0520
Phone: (609) 292-6259
Fax: (609) 984-7900
Web site: *www.njstatelib.org*

Ocean County Law Library
Justice Complex, Rm. 243
120 Hooper Ave.
Toms River, NJ 08754
Phone: (732) 929-2042
Web site: *www.judiciary.state.nj.us/ocean/index.htm*

*Seton Hall University
School of Law
Peter W. Rodino, Jr. Law Library
1 Newark Center
Newark, NJ 07102-5210
Phone: (973) 642-8861
Fax: (973) 642-8748
Web site: *http://law.shu.edu/library/index.html*
** restricted access to depository only**

*Rutgers University, Camden
Law School Library
217 N. 5th St.
Camden, NJ 08102
Phone: (856) 225-6173
Fax: (856) 225-6488
Web site: *http://lawlibrary.rutgers.edu*

*Rutgers University, Newark
Law Library
123 Washington St.
Newark, NJ 07102-3094
Phone: (973) 353-5676
Fax: (973) 353-1356
Web site: *http://law-library.rutgers.edu*

NEW MEXICO

*New Mexico Supreme Court
Law Library
237 Don Gaspar Ave.
Santa Fe, NM 87501
Phone: (505) 827-4850
Fax: (505) 827-4852
Web site: *http://fscll.org*

*University of New Mexico
School of Law Library
1117 Stanford Dr. Northeast
Albuquerque, NM 87131-1441
Phone: (505) 277-5131
Fax: (505) 277-0068
Web site: *http://lawschool.unm.edu/library/aboutlib.html*

NEW YORK

*Schaffer Law Library
Albany Law School
80 New Scotland Ave.
Albany, NY 12208-3494
Phone: (518) 445-2390
Fax: (518) 472-5842
Web site: *www.als.edu/lib*

*Arthur W. Diamond Law Library
Columbia Law School
435 W. 116th St.
New York, NY 10027
Phone: (212) 854-3743
Fax: (212) 854-3295
Web site: *www.law.columbia.edu/library*
** only access to federal depository materials for general public**

*Barbara & Maurice Deane
Law Library
Hofstra University School of Law
California Ave.
Hempstead, NY 11549
Phone: (516) 463-5898
Fax: (516) 463-5129
Web site: *www.hofstra.edu/libraries/
lawlib/law_library.cfm*
** only access to federal depository
materials for general public**

*Brooklyn Law School Library
250 Joralemon St.
Brooklyn, NY 11201
Phone: 718-780-7973
Fax: 718-780-0369
Web site: *http://brkl.brooklaw.edu*
** only access to federal depository
materials for general public**

*Charles B. Sears Law Library
State University of New York,
Buffalo
O'Brian Hall, Amherst Campus
Buffalo, NY 14260-1110
Phone: (716) 645-2047
Fax: (716) 645-3860
Web site: *http://ublib.buffalo.edu/
libraries/units/law*

*CUNY Law School Library
CUNY School of Law
at Queens College
65-21 Main St.
Flushing, NY 11367-1358
Phone: (718) 340-4240
Fax: (718) 340-4276
Web site: *www.law.cuny.edu/library*

*Cornell University Law Library
340 Myron Taylor Hall
Ithaca, NY 14853-4901
Phone: (607) 255-9577
Fax: (607) 255-1357
Web site: *www.lawschool.cornell.edu/
library*

*Chutick Law Library
Cardozo School of Law
Yeshiva University
55 5th Ave.
New York, NY 10003-4301
Phone: (212) 790-0220
Fax: (212) 790-0236
Web site: *www.cardozo.yu.edu/
library/index.html*
** only access to federal depository
materials for general public**

*H. Douglas Barclay Law Library
Syracuse University
E.I. White Hall
Syracuse, NY 13244-1030
Phone: (315) 443-9560
Fax: (315) 443-9567
Web site: *www.law.syr.edu/
lawlibrary/lawlibrary.asp*

* Leo T. Kissam Memorial Library
Fordham University School of Law
140 W. 62nd St.
New York, NY 10023
Phone: (212) 636-6908
Fax: (212) 636-7357
Web site: *www.fordham.edu/law/
lawlib/guide.htm*

*New York Law School Law Library
40 Washington Sq. South
New York, NY 10012-2115
Phone: (212) 998-6600
Fax: (212) 995-3477
Web site: *www.nyls.edu/
content.php?ID=81*

Pace University Law Library
78 N. Broadway
White Plains, NY 10603-3710
Phone: (914) 422-4273
Fax: (914) 422-4139
Web site: *http://csmail.law.pace.edu/
lawlib*

* Rittenberg Law Library
St. Johns University
8000 Utopia Pkwy.
Jamaica, NY 11439
Phone: (718) 990-1896
Fax: (718) 990-6649
Web site: *www.courts.state.ny.us/
queenslib/queens.htm*

* Jacob D. Fuchsberg
Law Center Library
Touro College
300 Nassau Rd.
Huntington, NY 11743
Phone: (631) 421-2244
Fax: (631) 421-2675
Web site: *www.tourolaw.edu/
abouttlc/Library*
** only access to federal depository
materials for general public**

New York State Supreme Court
Library, Buffalo
92 Franklin St., 4th Fl.
Buffalo, NY 14202
Phone: (716) 852-0712
Fax: (716) 852-3454
Web site: *www.courts.State.ny.us/8jd/
NYSSClawlib/NYSSCbuff.htm*

New York State Supreme Court
Library, Queens County
88-11 Sutphin Blvd., Rm. 600
Jamaica, NY 11435
Phone: (718) 520-3140
Fax: (718) 520-3589
Web site: *www.courts.state.ny.us/
queenslib/queens.htm*

Supreme Court of New York
Criminal Law Library
100 Centre St., 17th Fl.
New York, NY 10013
Phone: (212) 374-5882
Fax: (212) 748-7908
Web site: *www.courts.state.ny.us/
supctcrimlib1*

NORTH CAROLINA

Norman A. Wiggins
School of Law Library
Campbell University
P.O. Box 158
Buies Creek, NC 27506
Phone: (910) 893-1750
Web site: *http://webster.campbell.edu/
culawlib.htm*

*Duke University
School of Law Library
P.O. Box 90361
Towerview & Science Dr.
Durham, NC 27708-0361
Phone: (919) 613-7121
Fax: (919) 613-7237
Web site: *http://library.law.duke.edu*

* Kathrine R. Everett Law Library
University of North Carolina,
Chapel Hill
Van Hecke-Wettach Bldg., CB
#3385
Chapel Hill, NC 27599-3385
Phone: (919) 962-1194
Fax: (919) 962-2294
Web site: *http://library.law.unc.edu*

*North Carolina Central University
Law Library
1512 S. Alston Ave.
Durham, NC 27707
Phone: (919) 530-7175
Fax: (919) 530-7926
Web site: *www.nccu.edu/law/library/
index.html*

*North Carolina Supreme Court
Library
Justice Building
2 E. Morgan St.
Raleigh, NC 27601-1428
Phone: (919) 733-3425
Fax: (919) 733-0105
Web site: *www.aoc.state.nc.us/
www/public/html/sc_library.htm*

* Professional Center Library
Wake Forest University
1834 Wake Forest Rd.
P.O. Box 7206, Reynolda Station
Winston-Salem, NC 27109
Phone: (336) 758-4520
Fax: (336) 758-6077
Web site: *http://pcl.wfu.edu*

NORTH DAKOTA

*North Dakota Supreme Court
Law Library
Judicial Wing Capitol Bldg., 2nd Fl.
600 E. Boulevard Ave.
Bismarck, ND 58505-0530
Phone: (701) 328-2227
Fax: (701) 328-3609
Web site: *www.court.State.nd.us/
LawLib/www6.htm*

Thormodsgard Law Library
University of North Dakota
P.O. Box 9003
Grand Forks, ND 58202-9003
Phone: (701) 777-2104
Fax: (701) 777-6447
Web site: *www.law.und.nodak.edu/
lawweb/thormodsgard/library.html*

OHIO

Akron Law Library Association
209 S. High St., 4th Fl.
Akron, OH 44308-1675
Phone: (330) 643-2804
Fax: (330) 535-0077
Web site: *www.akronlawlib.org*
public must pay fee

Cincinnati Law Library Association
1000 Main St., Rm. 601
Cincinnati, OH 45202-1298
Phone: (513) 946-5300
Fax: (513) 946-5252
Web site: *www.hamilton-co.org/cinlawlib*
public must pay fee

Clermont County Law Library
Clermont County Courthouse
270 Main St.
Batavia, OH 45103
Phone: (513) 732-7109
Fax: (513) 732-0974
Web site: *www.cclla.org*

Cleveland Law Library Association
1 W. Lakeside Ave., 4th Fl.
Cleveland, OH 44113-1078
Phone: (216) 861-5070
Fax: (216) 861-1606
Web site: *www.clelaw.lib.oh.us*

Columbiana County Law Library
Columbiana County Courthouse
105 S. Market St.
Lisbon, OH 44432
Phone: (330) 420-3662
Fax: (330) 424-7902
Web site: *http://dragnet.epohi.com/~lawlib/lawlibrary*

The Columbus Law Library
369 S. High St., 10th Fl.
Columbus, OH 43215
Phone: (614) 221-4181
Fax: (614) 221-2115
Web site: *www.columbuslawlib.org*

The Crawford County
Law Library Association
112 E. Mansfield St., Ste. 90
Bucyrus, OH 44820
Phone: 419-562-7863
Fax: 419-562-2632
Web site: *http://cclla.crawford-co.org*

Butler County
Law Library Association
10 Journal Sq., Ste. 200
Hamilton, OH 45011
Phone: (513) 887-3455
Fax: (513) 887-3696
Web site: *www.bclawlib.org*

The Lorain County
Law Library Association
226 Middle Ave.
Elyria, OH 44035
Phone: (440) 329-5567
Fax: (440) 322-1724
Web site: *www.lorainlawlib.org*

Mahoning Law Library Association
Courthouse, 4th Fl.
120 Market St.
Youngstown, OH 44503-1752
Phone: (330) 740-2295
Fax: (330) 744-1406
Web site: *www.mahoninglawlibrary.org*

Stark County
Law Library Association
110 Central Plaza South, Ste. 401
Canton, OH 44702
Phone: (330) 451-7380
Fax: (330) 451-7381
Web site: *www.starklawlibrary.org*

Trumbull County Law Library
120 High St., NW
Warren, OH 44481
Phone: (330) 675-2525
Fax: (330) 675-2527
Web site: *www.trumbulllaw.org*

Capital University
School of Law Library
303 E. Broad St.
Columbus, OH 43215-3200
Phone: (614) 236-6464
Fax: (614) 236-6957
Web site: *www.law.capital.edu/
library*

*Case Western Reserve University
School of Law Library
11075 East Blvd.
Cleveland, OH 44106-7148
Phone: (216) 368-5206
Fax: (216) 368-1002
Web site: *http://lawwww.cwru.edu/
library*

*Cleveland-Marshall
College of Law Library
Cleveland State University
1801 Euclid Ave.
Cleveland, OH 44115-2403
Phone: (216) 687-6877
Fax: (216) 687-5098
Web site: *www.law.csuohio.edu/
lawlibrary*

*University of Toledo
College of Law Library
2801 W. Bancroft St.
Toledo, OH 43606-3390
Phone: (419) 530-2733
Fax: (419) 530-2821
Web site: *http://law.utoledo.edu/
lavalleylibrary/index.htm*

*Ohio State University
Mortiz Law Library
55 W. 12th Ave.
Columbus, OH 43210-1391
Phone: (614) 292-9463
Fax: (614) 292-3202
Web site: *www.osu.edu/units/law/
library.htm*

Marx Law Library
University of Cincinnati
College of Law
P.O. Box 210040
Cincinnati, OH 45221-0040
Phone: (513) 556-0159
Fax: (513) 556-6265
Web site: *www.law.uc.edu/library/
index.html*

*Ohio Northern University
Jay P. Taggart Law Library
439 S. Gilbert St.
Ada, OH 45810
Phone: (419) 772-2254
Fax: (419) 772-1875
Web site: *www.law.onu.edu/library/
default.htm*

* C. Blake McDowell Law Center
University of Akron
150 University Ave.
Akron, OH 44325-2902
Phone: (330) 972-7330
Fax: (330) 972-4948
Web site: *www.uakron.edu/law/
library/index.php*

*Supreme Court of Ohio
Rhodes State Office Tower
30 E. Broad St., 4th Fl.
Columbus, OH 43215-3431
Phone: (614) 466-1520
Fax: (614) 466-1559
Web site: *www.sconet.state.oh.us/
LawLibrary*

OKLAHOMA

* Dulaney-Browne Library
Oklahoma City University
2501 N. Blackwelder
Oklahoma City, OK 73106-1493
Phone: (405) 521-5073
Fax: (405) 521-5291
Web site: *www.okcu.edu/law/library/
main.asp*

Oklahoma County Law Library
321 Park Ave., Rm. 247
Oklahoma City, OK 73102
Phone: (405) 713-1353
Fax: (405) 713-1852
Web site: *www.oklahomacounty.org/
departments/lawlibrary/index.html*

*University of Tulsa
Mabee Legal Information Center
3120 E. 4th Pl.
Tulsa, OK 74104
Phone: (918) 631-2460
Fax: (918) 631-3556
Web site: *www.law.utulsa.edu/library*
public must pay fee

*Donald E. Pray Law Library
University of Oklahoma
300 Timberdell Rd.
Norman, OK 73019-5801
Phone: (405) 325-5268
Fax: (405) 325-6282
Web site: *www.law.ou.edu/library*

OREGON

John E. Jaqua Law Library
1221 University of Oregon
Eugene, OR 97403-1221
Phone: (541) 346-3088
Fax: (541) 346-1669
Web site: *http://lawlibrary.
uoregon.edu*

* J.W. Long Library
Willamette University
245 Winter St., SE
Salem, OR 97301
Phone: (503) 370-6386
Fax: (503) 375-5426
Web site: *www.willamette.edu/
law/longlib*

Boley Law Library
Lewis & Clark Law School
10015 S.W. Terwilliger Blvd.
Portland, OR 97219
Phone: (503) 768-6676
Web site: *www.lclark.edu/~lawlib*

*State of Oregon Law Library
1163 State St.
Salem, OR 97301-2563
Phone: (503) 986-5640
Fax: (503) 986-5623
Web site: *www.ojd.state.or.us/osca/
acs/lawlibrary/index.htm*

PENNSYLVANIA

*Duquesne University Law Library
600 Forbes Ave.
900 Locust St.
Pittsburgh, PA 15282-0205
Phone: (412) 396-5014
Fax: (412) 396-6294
Web site: *www.lawlib.duq.edu*

* Barco Law Library
University of Pittsburgh
3900 Forbes Ave.
Pittsburgh, PA 15260-0001
Phone: (412) 648-1325
Fax: (412) 648-1352
Web site: *www.law.pitt.edu/library*

Beaver County Law Library
Courthouse
810 3rd St.
Beaver, PA 15009
Phone: (724) 728-3934
Fax: (724) 728-4133
Web site: *http://co.beaver.pa.us/
lawlibrary*

*Biddle Law Library
University of Pennsylvania
3460 Chestnut St.
Philadelphia, PA 19104-6403
Phone: (215) 898-7853
Fax: (215) 898-6619
Web site: *www.law.upenn.edu/bll*

Bucks County Courts Law Library
Bucks County Courthouse, 1st Fl.
55 E. Court St.
Doylestown, PA 18901
Phone: (215) 348-6023
Fax: (215) 348-6827
Web site: *www.buckscounty.org/
courts/lawlibrary.html*

Butler County Law Library
County Courthouse, Lower Fl.
124 W. Diamond St.
P.O. Box 1208
Butler, PA 16003
Phone: (724) 284-5206
Fax: (724) 284-5210
Web site: *www.co.butler.pa.us/ll.htm*

Chester County Law Library
Bar Association Bldg.
15 W. Gay St., Ste. 300
West Chester, PA 19380-3014
Phone: (610) 344-6166
Web site: *www.chesco.org/*
lawlib.html

Dauphin County Law Library
101 Market St., 5th Fl.
Harrisburg, PA 17101
Phone: (717) 255-2797
Fax: (717) 255-2817
Web site: *www.dauphinc.org/*
courts/lawlibrary/lawlibrary.asp

Fayette County Law Library
Fayette County Courthouse
61 E. Main St.
Uniontown, PA 15401-3514
Phone: (724) 340-1228
Fax: (724) 340-4886
Web site: *www.lcsys.net/fayette/*
county/lawlib/lawlib.htm

Francis J. Catania Law Library
Media Courthouse
201 W. Front St.
Media, PA 19063
Phone: (610) 891-4462
Fax: (610) 891-4480
Web site: *www.delco.lib.pa.us/*
liblist./ll.html

Jenkins Law Library
833 Chestnut East, Ste. 1220
Philadelphia, PA 19107-4429
Phone: (215) 574-7900
Web site: *www.jenkinslaw.org*
$5 fee for nonlawyers

Lehigh County Law Library
455 W. Hamilton St.
Allentown, PA 18101
Phone: (610) 782-3385
Fax: (610) 820-3311
Web site: *www.lccpa.org/depts/*
lawlibrary.html

Lancaster County Law Library
50 N. Duke St.
P.O. Box 83480
Lancaster, PA 17608-3480
Phone: (717) 299-8090
Fax: (717) 295-2509
Web site: *www.co.lancaster.pa.us/*
courts/cwp/view.asp?a=473&Q=262
314&courtsNav=|6224|

Law Library of
Montgomery County
Courthouse
P.O. Box 311
Norristown, PA 19404-0311
Phone: (610) 278-3806
Fax: (610) 278-5998
Web site: *www.montcopa.org/llmc*

Lawrence County Law Library
430 Court St.
New Castle, PA 16101
Phone: (724) 656-2136
Fax: (724) 658-4489
Web site: *www.co.lawrence.pa.us/*
lawlibrary/index.html

*Legal Information Center
Widener University
School of Law Library
3800 Vartan Way
Harrisburg, PA 17106
Phone: (717) 541-3934
Web site: *www.law.widener.edu/
law-library*

Mercer County Law Library
Mercer County Courthouse, 3rd Fl.
305 Mercer County Courthouse
Mercer, PA 16137
Phone: (724) 662-3800
Fax: (724) 662 0620
Web site: *www.mcc.co.mercer.pa.us/
library*

Pulling Law Library
Villanova University School of Law
299 N. Spring Mill Rd.
Villanova, PA 19085
Phone: (610) 519-7000
Web site: *www.law.villanova.edu/
library*
** $25 daily fee for public**

Senate Library of Pennsylvania
157 Capitol Bldg.
Harrisburg, PA 17120-3055
Phone: (717) 787-6120
Fax: (717) 783-5021
Web site: *www.pasen.gov/senate_
library.html*

*Penn State Dickinson
School of Law
Sheely-Lee Law Library
150 S. College St.
Carlisle, PA 17013-2861
Phone: (717) 240-5267
Fax: (717) 240-5127
Web site: *www.dsl.psu.edu/library/
libhome.html#lr*

*Temple University
School of Law Library
1719 N. Broad St.
Philadelphia, PA 19122
Phone: (215) 204-7891
Fax: (215) 204-1785
Web site: *www2.law.temple.edu/
page.asp?page=library*
** only access to federal depository
materials for general public; call
ahead**

Westmoreland County Law Library
Westmoreland County Courthouse
2 N. Main St., Rm. 202
Greenburg, PA 15601
Phone: (724) 830-3042
Fax: (724) 830-3266
Web site: *www.co.westmoreland.
pa.us/crt/assocoff/lawlib.htm*

RHODE ISLAND

Ralph R. Papitto
Law School Library
Roger Williams University
10 Metacom Ave.
Bristol, RI 02809
Phone: (401) 254-4500
Fax: (401) 254-3525
Web site: *http://law.rwu.edu/lawlib/
index.html*

*The Rhode Island State
Law Library
Frank Licht Judicial Complex
250 Benefit St.
Providence, RI 02903
Phone: (401) 222-3275
Fax: (401) 222-3865
Web site: *www.courts.State.ri.us/
library/defaultlibrary.htm*

SOUTH CAROLINA

Coleman Karesh Law Library
University of South Carolina,
Columbia
Maine & Greene Sts.
Columbia, SC 29208-0001
Phone: (803) 777-5942
Fax: (803) 777-9405
Web site: *www.law.sc.edu/lawlib.htm*

SOUTH DAKOTA

McKusick Law Library
University of South Dakota
414 E. Clark
Vermillion, SD 57069
Phone: (605) 677-5259
Fax: (605) 677-5417
Web site: *www.usd.edu/lawlib*

TENNESSEE

*Massey Law Library
Vanderbilt University
131 21st Ave., South, Ste. 209
Nashville, TN 37203-1164
Phone: (615) 322-2838
Fax: (615) 343-7451
Web site: *http://law.vanderbilt.edu/
library*

*Joel A. Katz Law Library
University of Tennessee, Knoxville
1505 W. Cumberland Ave.
Knoxville, TN 37996-1800
Phone: (865) 974-4381
Fax: (865) 974-6571
Web site: *www.law.utk.edu/admin/
library/INDEX.htm*

*Humphreys School of Law Library
University of Memphis
3715 Central Ave.
Memphis, TN 38152
Phone: (901) 678-2426
Fax: (901) 678-5293
Web site: *www.law.memphis.edu/
library*

TEXAS

*Sheridan and John Eddie Williams
Legal Research Center
Baylor University
1114 S. University Parks Dr.
P.O. Box 97128
Waco, TX 76798-7128
Phone: (254) 710-2168
Fax: (254) 710-2294
Web site: *http://law.baylor.edu/
library/lib_general/index.htm*

Dell Dehay Law Library
of Tarrant County
100 W. Weatherford, Rm. 420
Fort Worth, TX 76196-0800
Phone: (817) 884-1481
Fax: (817) 884-1509
Web site: *http://portal2.tarrant
county.com/law_library/site/
default.asp*

*O'Quinn Law Library
University of Houston
12 Law Library
Houston, TX 77204-6054
Phone: (713) 743-2300
Fax: (713) 743-2299
Web site: *www.lawlib.uh.edu/libraries*

*Sarita Kenedy East Law Library
St. Mary's University
1 Camino Santa Maria
San Antonio, TX 78230
Phone: (210) 436-3435
Fax: (210) 436-3240
Web site: *www.stmarytx.edu/law/
index.php?group=library&page=
generic.php*

*The Fred Parks Law Library
South Texas College of Law
1303 San Jacinto St.
Houston, TX 77002-7000
Phone: (713) 646-1712
Fax: (713) 659-2217
Web site: *www.stcl.edu/library/
libhome.html*

*Texas State Law Library
Tom C. Clark Bldg.
205 W. 14th St.
P.O. Box 12367
Austin, TX 78711-2367
Phone: (512) 463-1722
Fax: (512) 463-1728
Web site: *www.sll.state.tx.us*

*Tarlton Law Library
University of Texas, Austin
727 E. Dean Keeton St.
Austin, TX 78705-5799
Phone: (512) 232-3805
Fax: (512) 471-0243
Web site: *http://tarlton.law.utexas.edu*

* Thurgood Marshall
School of Law Library
Texas Southern University
3100 Cleburne Ave.
Houston, TX 77004-4501
Phone: (713) 313-4472
Fax: (713) 313-4483
Web site: *www.tsulaw.edu*

*Texas Tech University Law Library
1802 Hartford Ave.
Lubbock, TX 79409-0004
Phone: (806) 742-3957
Fax: (806) 742-1629
Web site: *www.law.ttu.edu/
lawlibrary*

UTAH

* Howard W. Hunter Law Library
Brigham Young University
260 JRC Blvd.
Provo, UT 84602-8000
Phone: (801) 422-6658
Fax: (801) 422-0404
Web site: *www.law.byu.edu/
law_library*

* S.J. Quinn Law Library
University of Utah
332 S.1400 East
Salt Lake City, UT 84112-0731
Phone: (801) 581-6184
Fax: (801) 585-3033
Web site: *www.law.utah.edu/library*

Utah State Law Library
Scott M. Matheson Courthouse
450 South State St., 1st Fl.
P.O. Box 140220
Salt Lake City, UT 84114-0220
Phone: (801) 238-7990
Fax: (801) 238-7993
Web site: *www.utcourts.gov/courts/
appell/lawlib.htm*

Weber County Law Library
2464 Jefferson Ave.
Ogden, UT 84401-1412
Phone: (801) 337-8466
Fax: (801) 337-2615
Web site: *www.weberpl.lib.ut.us/
law.htm*

VIRGINIA

Alexandria Law Library
520 King St., Rm. L-34
Alexandria, VA 22314
Phone: (703) 838-4077
Fax: (703) 838-5055
Web site: *www.alexandrialaw
library.org*

Appalachian School of Law Library
Rt. 5, P.O. Box 450
Grundy, VA 24614
Phone: (276) 935-6688
Fax: (276) 935-7138
Web site: *www.asl.edu/library*

*Arthur J. Morris Law Library
University of Virginia
580 Massie Rd.
Charlottesville, VA 22903-1789
Phone: (434) 924-3504
Fax: (434) 982-2232
Web site: *www.law.virginia.edu/
libitc.htm*

*George Mason University
Law Library
3301 N. Fairfax Dr.
Arlington, VA 22201-4426
Phone: (703) 993-8120
Fax: (703) 993-8113
Web site: *www.gmu.edu/
departments/law/libtech*

* Marshall-Wythe School of Law
Library
William and Mary University
S. Henry St.
P.O. Box 8795
Williamsburg, VA 23187-8795
Phone: (757) 221-3255
Fax: (757) 221-3051
Web site: *www.wm.edu/law/
lawlibrary/index.php*

Regent University
School of Law Library
1000 Regent University Dr.
Virginia Beach, VA 23464-9800
Phone: (757) 226-4450
Fax: (757) 226-4451
Web site: *www.regent.edu/acad/
schlaw/library*

*Supreme Court of Virginia State
Law Library
100 N. 9th St.
Richmond, VA 23219-2335
Phone: (804) 786-2075
Fax: (804) 786-4542
Web site: *www.courts.state.va.us/
library/library.htm*

*Wilbur C. Hall Law Library
Washington and Lee University
Lexington, VA 24450-0303
Phone: (540) 463-8544
Fax: (540) 463-8967
Web site: *http://law.wlu.edu/library*

*Muse Law Library
University of Richmond
Richmond, VA 23173
Phone: (804) 289-8685
Fax: (804) 289-8683
Web site: *http://law.richmond.edu/
library/musehome.htm*

WASHINGTON

*Chastek Law Library
Gonzaga University School of Law
721 N. Cincinnati St.
Spokane, WA 99220
Phone: (509) 323-5792
Web site: *http://law.gonzaga.edu/
library/index.htm*

*King County Law Library
Administrative Bldg., Rm. 807
500 4th Ave.
Seattle, WA 98104
Phone: (206) 296-0940
Web site: *www.kcll.org*

Kitsap County Law Library
614 Division St.
Port Orchard, WA 98366
Phone: (360) 337-5788
Web site: *www.kitsapbar.com/library*

*Marian Gould Gallagher
Law Library
University of Washington
School of Law
1100 N.E. Campus Pkwy.
Seattle, WA 98105-6617
Phone: (206) 543-4086
Web site: *http://lib.law.
washington.edu*

*Seattle University School of Law
900 Broadway
Seattle, WA 98122-4340
Phone: (206) 398-4225
Fax: (206) 398-4194
Web site: *www.law.seattleu.edu/
library?mode=standard*
$5 day pass for public

Spokane County Law Library
421 W. Riverside Ave.
Paulsen Bldg., Ste. 1020
Spokane, WA 99201
Phone: (509) 477-3680
Fax: (509) 477-4722
Web site: *www.spokanecounty.org/
lawlibrary/default.asp*

Washington State Law Library
Temple of Justice
P.O. Box 40751, AV-02
Olympia, WA 98504-0751
Phone: (360) 357-2136
Fax: (360) 357-2143
Web site: *www.courts.wa.gov/library*

WASHINGTON, D.C.

*Allen Mercer Daniel Law Library
Howard University School of Law
2900 Van Ness St., NW
Washington, D.C. 20008
Phone: (202) 806-8045
Web site: *www.law.howard.edu/
library*

*Edward Bennett Williams
Law Library
Georgetown University
School of Law
111 G St., NW
Washington, DC 20001
Phone: (202) 662-9131
Web site: *www.ll.georgetown.edu*
**Only access to federal depository
materials for general public**

*Judge Kathryn J. DuFour
Law Library
The Catholic University of America
3600 John McCormack Rd., NE
Washington, DC 20064
Phone: (202) 319-5155
Fax: (202) 319-5581
Web site: *http://law.cua.edu/library*

*Law Library of Congress
James Madison Bldg., Rm. LM-201
101 Independence Ave., SE
Washington, DC 20540-3129
Phone: (202) 707-5079
Fax: (202) 707-1820
Web site: *www.lcweb.loc.gov/rr/law*

*Washington College of Law
Library
American University
4801 Massachusetts Ave., NW
Washington, DC 20016-8182
Phone: (202) 274-4350
Fax: (202) 274-4365
Web site: *http://library.wcl.
american.edu*

WEST VIRGINIA

*West. Virginia Supreme Court of
Appeals State Law Library
State Capitol Bldg., Rm. E-404
1900 Kanawha Blvd., East
Charleston, WV 25305
Phone: (304) 558-2607
Fax: (304) 558-3673
Web site: *www.state.wv.us/wvsca/
library/menu.htm*

West Virginia University
College of Law Library
One Law Center Dr.
P.O. Box 6135
Morgantown, WV 26505-6135
Phone: (304) 293-5300
Fax: (304) 293-6020
Web site: *www.wvu.edu/~law/library/
library.html*

WISCONSIN

*Marquette University Law Library
Sensenbrenner Hall
1103 W. Wisconsin Ave.
P.O. Box 3137
Milwaukee, WI 53201-3137
Phone: (414) 288-6767
Fax: (414) 288-0676
Web site: *http://law.marquette.edu/
cgi-bin/site.pl*

*University of Wisconsin
Law Library
975 Bascom Mall
Madison, WI 53706
Phone: (608) 262-1128
Fax: (608) 262-2775
Web site: *http://library.law.wisc.edu*

*Wisconsin State Law Library
120 Martin Luther King, Jr. Blvd.,
2nd Fl.
Madison, WI 53703
Phone: (608) 267-9696
Fax: (608) 267-2319
Web site: *http://wsll.state.wi.us*

WYOMING

*George W. Hopper Law Library
UW College of Law
P.O. Box 3035
Laramie, WY 82071
Phone: (307) 766-2210
Fax: (307) 766-4044
Web site: *http://uwadmnweb.
uwyo.edu/law/lawlib/lawlib.htm*

*Wyoming State Law Library
2301 Capitol Ave.
Cheyenne, WY 82002-0060
Phone: (307) 777-7509
Fax: (307) 777-7240
Web site: *http://courts.state.wy.us/
fedlegal.htm*

Appendix V

Summary of Research Tools

This appendix briefly describes the types of sources discussed throughout this manual. As you read this appendix, it will be helpful to refer to the relevant parts of the manual for additional information about the sources and how to use them.

LAWYER HANDBOOKS

If you can find one on your area of legal concern, a lawyer's handbook might provide one-stop shopping. These are written by veteran lawyers for new lawyers in the field. Many are geared toward litigating cases, but some also answer commonly-asked research questions. Lawyer handbooks can be found in some law libraries, but many are only provided to members of certain issue-specific bar associations, such as a patent or immigration bar. An example is the *District of Columbia Practice Manual* published by the District of Columbia Bar.

LEGAL DICTIONARIES

Legal dictionaries, which define and explain thousands of legal terms, are used exactly as their plain-language counterparts. They come in two kinds: some for lawyers, such as *Black's Law Dictionary,* and others in plain language. Almost any bookstore will have at least one plain-language legal dictionary, such as *The Dictionary of Legal Terms, Real Life Dictionary of the Law* and *Random House Webster's Dictionary of the Law.* Every law library will at least have *Black's.*

LEGAL ENCYCLOPEDIAS

These multi-volume sets are probably the most accessible secondary research source. They are organized alphabetically by category and sub-category, and some include cross-references and bibliographies that can lead you directly to the answers and primary sources you're looking for. They also contain exhaustive indexes. At least one kind of legal encyclopedia can be found in every law library, and even some regular university and public libraries carry them. Among the most widely-used encyclopedias are the *Corpus Juris Secundum (C.J.S.)*, published by West Publishing Company, *American Jurisprudence (Am. Jur.)* and *American Law Reports (A.L.R.)*, both published by Lawyers Co-operative Publishing Company. Don't forget to check legal encyclopedias produced by self-help legal publishers such as *Quicken Lawyer Personal*. They often cover a variety of legal issues and supply forms and instructions for completing simple legal tasks.

LOOSE-LEAF SERVICES

Loose-leaf services provide a host of research material, including case law, statutory law and administrative law. They are updated regularly (often weekly) and function as reporters organized by subject matter rather than by jurisdiction, as case reporters are. These publications allow you to maintain an up-to-the-minute understanding of a particular area of law. Some kinds are carried by every law library. For a complete list, see Appendix III.

TREATISES OR HORNBOOKS

Treatises, or *hornbooks,* are written by legal experts and cover an entire body of law, such as contracts, civil procedure or wills and trusts. They usually are published in a single volume, although some consist of several volumes. Like school textbooks, they detail every aspect of the law taught in law school. Loaded with case law, most are written for law students and lawyers. Some, however, particularly the introductory texts, explain general concepts of law. A few examples are *Torts,* by William Prosser, and *Contracts,* by Calamari and Perillo. Others are paperbacks called *Nutshells* or *Black Letter Series,* published by West. Titles include *Constitutional Law, Workers' Compensation and Employee Protection Laws* and *Administrative Law.*

LAW JOURNALS

Seasonal law journals, typically published by law schools or lawyers' trade associations, cover specialized areas of law, such as tax law or international law. Others are more general. Many of the articles are written by legal scholars and law professors. Although some are on arcane points of law, many others summarize the case law on a certain point with footnotes that can lead you to primary sources.

FORM BOOKS

Form books are collections of sample forms used in legal transactions, such as standard contracts, power-of-attorney agreements, pleadings and other court papers. Almost all lawyers use them in drafting legal documents. They come in two types: general (for all aspects of legal practice) and subject-related (for a single topic or area of law). In addition to giving you sample forms and procedural tips, they also give an idea of the kinds of documents that can be used to meet your legal needs. *American Jurisprudence Form Books* and *West's Form Books* are two of the more general ones in use. Do-it-yourself legal form books, kits and software programs are also available *(see Appendix VI)*.

PRACTICE AND PROCEDURE BOOKS

These are like form books but put greater emphasis on drafting the documents needed for a court case and for understanding the procedure in a certain jurisdiction. Some are geared for federal court practice, others for a specific state practice. They help mostly with procedural matters but can also help answer substantive legal questions. They are a must for anyone involved in litigation. Examples of state practice and procedure books are *Michies on Virginia Practice* and *Goodrich and Amram on Pennsylvania Practice*. Federal practice books include *American Jurisprudence* and West's series.

FEDERAL CODES

United States Code (U.S.C.)
United States Code Annotated (U.S.C.A.)
United States Code Service (U.S.C.S.)

The *United State Code (U.S.C.)* is the official code of laws enacted by the U.S. Congress. It includes all the laws in effect up to the current Congress. The *United States Code Annotated (U.S.C.A.)* and the *United States Code Service (U.S.C.S.)* are the unofficial series of volumes that include not only the actual laws of Congress but also related case law and articles that deal with the statutes. All are organized by subject and can be found in most law libraries.

STATE CODES

Each state has its own printed code of laws. These usually are organized just as the *U.S.C.* Some states also have unofficial code services that, like the *U.S.C.A.* and *U.S.C.S.*, include relevant cases and articles.

ADMINISTRATIVE CODES

Executive agencies print their rules and regulations in administrative codes. At the federal level, rules are found in the *Code of Federal Regulations (CFR)*. State agencies also publish their rules in state administrative codes, or if the state lacks such a code, in the state's register of regulations.

REPORTERS

Case decisions from the highest court and appellate courts are published in state and regional reporters. Federal cases are published in federal reporters. Cases are published in chronological order, with newer cases printed in paperback form until they can be collected in bound volumes. Reporters are impossible to use with any efficiency unless you use an encyclopedia, digest or some other secondary source to direct you to cases relevant to your research.

DIGESTS

Digests are collections of short descriptions of cases organized by subject. They include state-specific digests, regional digests, federal law digests and digests that combine all of these. They collect all of the case law for certain jurisdictions on the same subject. Their pocket parts ensure that what you are reading is the most recent information. Almost all law libraries subscribe to at least one digest service.

SHEPARD'S CITATIONS

These volumes tell you if a case or statute you are relying on has been overturned, upheld or referred to by another court. *Sheparatizing* a case is of critical importance before you rely on the case's holdings. Shepard's provides both a coded method of checking the present validity of the law that you are citing and leads you to other cases that have discussed the decision you are concerned with.

Self-help Law

Today many Americans are getting answers to their legal questions without having to consult an attorney or step into a law library. They're turning instead to the Internet and the ever-increasing number of do-it-yourself legal books, kits and software programs that are on the market. For simple, straightforward questions or concerns, this approach may be far better than turning to a law library.

This appendix lists some of the better-known publishers of self-help legal material. It's not an exhaustive list and other publishers, like Random House or John Wiley & Sons, also carry self-help titles from time to time. If the publishers below do not carry the information you're looking for, you can also research the topic online (perhaps through a book seller like *Amazon.com*) or check *Books in Print* at your local bookstore.

You might also find answers to your questions and sample legal forms in the listing of *Pro Se Resources* and *Pro Se Centers* (reprinted from HALT's *Citizens Legal Manual,* **The Legal Resource Directory: Your Guide to Help, Hotlines & Hot Websites).**

SELF-HELP PUBLISHERS

ALLWORTH PRESS
10 E. 23rd St., Ste. 510
New York, NY 10010
Phone: (212) 777-8395
Fax: (212) 777-8261
E-Mail: *PUB@allworth.com*
Web site: *www.allworth.com*

HALT, INC.
1612 K St., NW, Ste. 510
Washington, DC 20006
Phone: (202) 887-8255
Fax: (202) 887-9699
E-Mail: *halt@halt.org*
Web site: *www.halt.org*

NOLO
950 Parker St.
Berkeley, CA 94710-2524
Toll free: (800) 728-3555
Toll free fax: (800) 645-0895
E-Mail: *cs@nolo.com*
Web site: *www.nolo.com*

NOVA PUBLISHING
1103 West College St.
Carbondale, IL 62901
Toll free: (800) 462-6420
Toll free fax: (800) 338-4550
E-Mail: *info@novapublishing.com*
Web site: *www.novapublishing.com*

ROUND LAKE PUBLISHING
P.O. Box 1084
Ridgefield, CT 06877
Phone: (203) 438-6303
Fax: (203) 431-6811
Web site: *www.letterworks.com*

SPHINX PUBLISHING
(a Division of Sourcebooks, Inc.)
P.O. Box 372
Naperville, IL 60566
Phone: (630) 961-3900
Fax: (630) 961-2168
Web site: *www.sourcebooks.com*

SELF-COUNSEL PRESS, INC.
1704 N. State St.
Bellingham, WA 98255
Phone: (360) 676-4530
Fax: (360) 676-4549
Toll free: (877) 877-6490
E-mail: *orderdesk@self-counsel.com*
Web site: *www.self-counsel.com*

PRO SE RESOURCES

This section lists the burgeoning resources available to those interested in going *pro se* (representing themselves). Here you will find commercial Web sites and *pro se* law centers.

COMMERCIAL WEB SITES

You can buy a lot of good (and not so good) things over the Internet. The same is true for legal services—be it advice, legal forms or legal products. The following is a sample list of commercial providers who have created Web sites to sell you something—typically their "legal" advice, books, software, kits or specific forms. New and similar Web sites are appearing all the time. Most include a fair amount of "free" legal information and simple free legal forms to go along with their sale items.

Before using any one Web site, it's a good idea to browse around and see what each one has to offer. You can get a feel for how detail-oriented the Web sites are by visiting more than one and comparing notes. Some will allow you to create your own state-specific legal form. Others ask you to fill out a questionnaire, and they will create the form for you.

All About Forms.com
Web site: *www.selfhelplaw.com*
This Web site offers more than 2,000 free legal forms and answers to common legal and financial questions. The site encourages people to join for 90 days ($24.95 in 2003) to gain access to their attorneys (unlimited free consultations) and a free downloaded copy of *Quicken Lawyer (Year) Personal Deluxe.* If you don't cancel your membership, you'll be billed $8.95 monthly.

AllLaw.com

Web site: *www.alllaw.com*

AllLaw.com includes articles, links and free legal forms on criminal and civil legal issues. Topics include: family law, estate planning, intellectual property, business, employment, criminal, tax, bankruptcy and more. The AllLaw site also includes a searchable database of lawyers and features a "lawyer of the week."

American Pro Se Association

Web site: *www.legalhelp.org*

American Pro Se Association is a non-profit, volunteer organization whose mission is to help people with financial and legal problems or questions. Basic information is free to the public and members who pay have access to Approved Legal Advisors and additional information on various financial and legal subjects.

Divorce Helpline

Web site: *www.divorcehelp.com*

Divorce Helpline provides information and help on out-of-court California divorces. A variety of services are offered, including attorney consultations, mediation sessions, collaborative divorces or a Complete Divorce Package, which the helpline helps you fill it out. The site also features articles, a short divorce course, recommended publications (both books and software) and a toll free number (1-800-359-7004).

Divorcelawinfo.com

Web site: *www.divorcelawinfo.com*

The Divorce Law Information Center is owned by licensed attorney Richard S. Granat who has hands-on experience in helping pro se litigants in family law matters. Since 1997, the center has helped thousands of couples do their own divorces. Links on the Web site send you to state-specific information on divorce, child support calculators, custody and visitation information and divorce and marital separation agreements.

Law Made Easy Press

Web site: *www.laweasy.com*

Law Made Easy Press is hosted by New Jersey lawyer and author Martin Shenkman. The Web site provides information on tax, estate, divorce, real estate and financial planning. Also included are links to audio clips from the Law Made Easy radio show, free legal forms and other features to help keep you informed.

LegalAdviceLine.com
Web site: *www.legaladviceline.com*

Legal Advice Line is a law firm online that helps you represent yourself in routine matters, reviews executed legal documents, prepares legal documents for you and helps you through a variety of situations including court hearings, negotiations or mediation with a unique brand of unbundled legal services. The site includes a toll free number (1-888-367-5252).

Marylandlawonline.com
Web site: *www.marylandlawonline.com*

Maryland Law Online is designed to provide detailed legal information on Maryland law that affects the average person or small business on a daily basis. It specializes in providing online legal forms, legal information, tools and services that enable you to either represent yourself as a pro se litigant or become a more effective purchaser of legal services. While this site is published and edited by attorneys who are members of the Maryland bar, they are not a law firm and are not supported by any lawyer advertising.

Nolo.com
Web site: *www.nolo.com*

From the premiere publisher of do-it-yourself legal materials, Nolo's Web site offers a huge selection of law-related articles in plain language. If you don't get your answers from the free stuff, you can order more comprehensive books and software to do your own legal work. You can also, for a fee, download electronic form kits or fill out a single legal form online.

The Pro Se Law Center
Web site: *www.pro-selaw.org*

The Pro Se Law Center is not a commercial site but it is useful to pro se litigants. The Pro Se Law Center is a resource center for collecting research and evaluating reports of pro se approaches to providing access to legal services. It provides a searchable directory of pro se programs, links to court pro se Web sites and a discussion forum for organizations that want to create a pro se assistance program.

USlegalforms.com

Web site: *www.uslegalforms.com*

U.S. Legal Forms offers thousands of legal forms. Many are related to business or litigating in Federal court. Others cover the typical range of legal topics including real estate, name change, wills, premarital agreements and promissory notes. Forms are available to attorneys, the public and businesses directly over the Internet. The Web site lists a toll free number (1-877-389-0141).

PRO SE CENTERS

The following is a list of *pro se* centers. Some are run by local courts, others by law schools or private organizations. Most are designed specifically to help *pro se* litigants—people who have chosen to represent themselves in court. The following is just a sampling of the centers that exist. Many more state courts are in the process of creating self-help centers to help the ever-increasing number of *pro se* litigants in this country. To see if a center has been created in your state, visit the American Bar Association Web site: *www.abanet.org/legalservices/publicinfo.html.*

Arizona

Self-Service Center

Web site: *www.superiorcourt.maricopa.gov/ssc/sschome.html*

The Web site for the Self-Service Center (a program of the Supreme Court of Arizona in Maricopa County), which was designed to help people help themselves in court. The site features general information on a variety of topics, court forms and instructions, and lists of lawyers and mediators who will help by providing expert advice.

Delaware

Delaware Self-Help Center

Web site: *www.courts.state.de.us/superior/prose.htm*

This Web site is hosted by the Superior Court of Delaware. It includes information on using Delaware courts, has a FAQ section, commonly-requested Superior Court forms and information about their e-courtroom and e-filing and docketing. Delaware was the first state in the nation to experiment with filing court forms over the Internet. More than 100,000 documents have been filed electronically in the Superior Court.

Hawaii
Hawaii's Self-Help Center
Web site: *www.courts.state.hi.us/index.jsp*
The Hawaii Self-Help Center's Web site offers general information on Hawaii's judiciary, downloadable court forms, links to legal references, services and attorneys. The site also links people to LawLine, a community service of the Hawaii State Bar and State Judiciary. People are given a number to call to receive free-recorded messages on various legal topics.

Illinois
Self-Help Law Legal Center
Web site: *www.law.siu.edu/selfhelp/index.htm*
The Self-Help Legal Center provides assistance to the institutions that come into contact with pro se litigants. It also helps *pro se* litigants directly by helping them find the information they need and it acts as a clearinghouse for self-help legal information. The site is sponsored by the Southern Illinois University School of Law.

Maine
Help Me Law
Web site: *www.helpmelaw.org/HML/About*
Help Me Law provide legal information for low-income people in the state of Maine. This includes easy-to-read self-help information on topics such as divorce and tenants rights, Medicaid and food stamps, as well as information about free and low-cost legal services in Maine. Links to other Maine legal service providers are also included.

Maryland
The People's Law Library of Maryland
Web site: *www.peoples-law.com*
The People's Law Library provides explanations of legal subjects, step-by-step procedures, legal forms and other legal information resources for the citizens of Maryland. The Web site is sponsored by the Maryland Legal Assistance Network.

Washington
Northwest Justice Project
Web site: *www.nwjustice.org*
The Northwest Justice Project's (NJP) Web site serves as a clearinghouse of legal self-help materials and tools that provide information about non-criminal legal problems affecting low-income people in Washington state. To learn whether you qualify for free assistance, contact the CLEAR hotline at 1-888-201-1014, or in King County, call (206) 464-1519; TTY 1-888-201-9737. NJP is a not-for-profit statewide organization that provides free civil legal services to low-income people from nine offices throughout the state of Washington.

About HALT

ALT—*An Organization of Americans for Legal Reform* is a national, non-profit, non-partisan public interest group of more than 50,000 members. It is dedicated to helping all Americans handle their legal affairs simply, affordably and equitably. HALT pursues an ambitious education and advocacy program to improve the quality, reduce the cost and increase the accessibility of the civil legal system.

Through five complementary reform projects, HALT is fighting to increase consumer choice in the marketplace and to strengthen protections against unscrupulous lawyers.

- *The Legal Consumers Bill of Rights* empowers consumers by providing the basic information they need when hiring a lawyer.
- *The Small Claims Reform Project* works to expand and strengthen the one-court system that actually benefits ordinary Americans.
- *The Freedom of Legal Information Project* fights to protect the rights of all Americans to use self-help law materials and non-traditional legal service providers.
- *The Lawyer Accountability Project* exposes lawyer misconduct and ensures that consumers have a voice in attorney discipline.
- *The Judicial Integrity Project* advocates for public oversight to prevent financial conflicts of interest and other ethical lapses by federal and state judges.

To achieve its goals, HALT publishes *Citizens Legal Manuals* like this one and an *Everyday Law Series* of brief legal guides to increase consumers' ability to handle their own legal affairs and help them become better-informed users of the legal system. Written in easy-to-understand language, these materials explain basic legal principles and procedures and include step-by-step instructions.

HALT's quarterly publication *The Legal Reformer* is the only national periodical of legal reform news and analysis. It informs readers about major legal reform developments and what they can do to help.

HALT activities are funded through member contributions and foundation support.

Join HALT

HALT accomplishes its mission through the generous support of its 50,000 members. We invite your participation.

❏ *Yes!*

I want to help reform America's civil justice system.
Enclosed is a check for my membership dues of:

❏ $25 *(minimum)*   ❏ $100
❏ $35   ❏ $250
❏ $50   ❏ $500

Or, please charge my contribution to:

❏ Visa   ❏ Mastercard   ❏ American Express

Credit Card No. _____

Expiration date _____

Signature _____

Name _____

Address _____

City/State/Zip_____

Phone _____

E-mail _____

Benefits of HALT Membership

- A free copy of **Using a Lawyer: And What To Do If Things Go Wrong**
- Action Alerts reporting on legal reform developments in your state
- HALT's quarterly newsletter *The Legal Reformer*
- A voice for your concerns about the lack of accessibility and affordability of America's civil justice system

1612 K Street, NW, Suite 510 • Washington, DC 20006
(202) 887-8255 • (202) 887-9699 fax
E-mail: *halt@halt.org* • *www.halt.org*